W9-CRK-723

Mountain Patterns

Mountain

Patterns

THE SURVIVAL OF NUOSU

CULTURE IN CHINA

STEVAN HARRELL

BAMO QUBUMO

and MA ERZI

Photographs by Zhong Dakun

UNIVERSITY OF WASHINGTON PRESS

Seattle and London

Copyright © 2000 by the University of Washington Press
Printed in the United States of America

Library of Congress Cataloging-in-Publication Data

Harrell, Stevan.
    Mountain patterns : the survival of Nuosu culture in China /
Stevan Harrell, Bamo Qubumo, and Ma Erzi; photographs by
Zhong Dakun.
       p. cm.
  ISBN 0-295-97937-2 (pbk. : alk. paper)
  1. Yi (Chinese people)—Social life and customs. 2. China,
Southwest—Civilization. I. Bamo, Qubumo. II. Ma, Erzi.
III. Title.
  DS731.N82 H37 2000
  951'.4—DC21   99-050681

Unless otherwise noted, photographs are by Zhong Dakun.

Front cover illustration: Leibo skirt (pl. 15). *Back cover:* Yynuo
rooster-style child's hat.

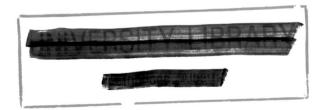

Contents

Acknowledgments

THIS VOLUME SERVES AS A COMPANION VOLUME TO the *Mountain Patterns* exhibit, presented at the Burke Museum of Natural History and Culture at the University of Washington from March through June 2000. Beyond that specific use, however, it constitutes an independent, illustrated introduction to Nuosu material culture. Much of the information presented here comes from the authors' personal experience and research: two of us grew up in Nuosu society (one in a village and one in a city), and all of us have conducted extensive field research in many parts of the Nuosu homeland. There is very little scholarship on Nuosu culture available in English; much of the Chinese scholarship is in obscure and unpublished journals. Thus, to make the text flow smoothly, we have dispensed with footnotes and bibliographic citations. Readers interested in pursuing research on any topic pertaining to Nuosu culture should contact the authors for bibliographic help. A forthcoming monograph by Stevan Harrell on ethnicity in Liangshan will include material on the Nuosu.

Chapters 1 and 4 were written in English; the others, originally written in Chinese, were translated into English by Stevan Harrell. All contain extensive Nuosu vocabulary, written in a modification of the standard Nuosu romanization system adopted for pedagogical and linguistic purposes. In this book, extra letters at the end of each syllable indicating tones have been omitted in order to make pronunciation easier for the general reader.

The publication of this volume was made possible by two generous grants from the China Studies Program of the University of Washington. The *Mountain Patterns* exhibit was made possible by grants from the Blakemore Foundation, the Asian Cultural Council, the Walter Chapin Simpson Center for the Humanities at the University of Washington, and the China Studies Program of the University of Washington.

We have had the help of an immense number of people in preparing this book.

For access to materials, we thank the staffs of the Liangshan Slave Society Museum, the Burke Museum of Natural History and Culture (particularly Becky Andrews, John Putnam, and Nicole Nathan), and Bamo Erha.

For help with the arcana of translating technical terms about material culture from Chinese into English, we would like to credit Deborah Harrell, Barbara B. Harrell, Helen Wattley-Ames, Bill Ames, Mary Hu, Lin Shin-hui, and Francesca Rebollo-Sborgi.

For help with Nuosu-language terminology and romanization, we are indebted to Wu Jingzhong.

For aid in transoceanic communication and coordination of a team of otherwise uncoordinated people, we are particularly grateful to Bamo Erha and Bamo Ayi.

For vision, precision, accuracy, optimism, good common sense, and the patience of Job, we are most thankful to Naomi Pascal, Lorri Hagman, and Veronica Seyd of the University of Washington Press.

Mountain Patterns

CHAPTER 1

The Survival of Nuosu Culture

STEVAN HARRELL

FOR A LONG TIME, THE CHINESE HAVE CALLED THE place Liangshan—the Cool Mountains—where the winters bring frost, cold winds, and sometimes snow to the steep slopes, the deep valleys, and the bare mountaintops. But to the Nuosu, the people who have lived there for a thousand years or more, it is just Nuosu Muddi or Nimu, the land of the Nuosu, where their existence was almost entirely autonomous until fifty years ago, and where their distinctive culture has evolved and survived to the present despite repeated attempts by outsiders to absorb or assimilate them.

The land of the Nuosu is as rugged as the people. It stands between the plains, hills, and medium-elevation plateaus of the Chinese provinces of Sichuan, eastern Yunnan, and Guizhou on the east and south, and the high peaks, deep valleys, and high grasslands of the Tibetan highlands on the west. Nimu, the land in between, does not yield up a living easily. Swift rivers, good for occasional fishing but not much else, run between a few narrow plains and the steep slopes that stretch toward the sky (fig. 1.1). Only a lucky few can live and farm on flat land. Most people live in isolated houses or small village clusters clinging to the mountainsides, building their dwellings out of whatever materials are available locally—wooden boards or planks, piled stones, or packed mud for walls; and straw thatch, wood shingles held down by rocks, or sometimes overlapping stone slabs for roofs. Floors are nothing but packed dirt, and furniture is simple, with home life centering around the floor hearth.

1.1. The Yalong River in Yanyuan County. (Photo by Stevan Harrell)

Around their simple dwellings, Nuosu have traditionally lived by a mixture of farming and herding. Their land for the most part has always been too high above sea level, and thus too cold, to grow the wet rice that is the staple of lowland peoples, but they gladly eat rice when and where they can get it. Most of the time, however, they have had to rely on coarser grains—corn and wheat in the middle elevations, oats on the highest slopes, and potatoes and buckwheat just about everywhere. A day's fare often consists only of potatoes, roasted in the hearth fire and peeled by hand, accompanied by pickled vegetable soup and perhaps dipped in hot peppers (fig. 1.2). Nuosu agriculture has never been very productive, and for that reason the population is scattered much more sparsely on the land than are the Han Chinese in the lowlands.

But land unsuitable for farming means plenty of pasture. Nuosu have always kept horses for transport and as work animals, or for the sheer pleasure of displaying and racing them; cattle for work and also to eat; and sheep, goats, chickens, and pigs for wool, meat, and eggs. Meat, however, is usually restricted to special occasions—weddings, funerals, holidays, or anytime unexpected guests came from far away. On those occasions, hospitality declares that "four legs" be slaughtered, the minimum offering being a pair of chickens. The offering of a pig expresses more respect for the occasion or the guest, a sheep or goat is still more special, and slaughter of an ox is the highest tribute that can be paid to the importance of the company or the solemnity of the occasion.

1.2. Children roasting and eating potatoes. (Photo by Stevan Harrell)

1.3. An ideal house site. (Photo by Stevan Harrell)

The piles of grain are like mountains.
We come to the stream at the side of the house to catch fish;
The fish are like piles of firewood.

The patterns are thus inseparable from the mountains themselves: intricately woven and embroidered skirts, tops, headpieces, and felt or fringed capes made from sheep's wool or from the hemp grown on the mountainsides (pl. 1); elaborately painted dishes and bowls, turned from native woods or bent from buffalohide and colored with local vegetable and mineral pigments in black, red, and yellow; silver and gold, mined locally or traded for local products, pounded thin by artisans who have learned their craft from generations of clan ancestors; songs and poems about bravery, beauty, fate, and loss, played on instruments manufactured from bamboo, wood, reeds, and other products of the hills; and ritual and ceremonial texts, written in the Nuosu's own script, explaining the mysteries of life and death, gods and ghosts, and the earth and sky of the mountain environment (fig. 1.4).

Throughout their history, Nuosu have responded to their stark environment by evolving a rich material and spiritual culture in harmony with the harsh surroundings. Ritual, ceremony, poetry, vocal and instrumental music, and the variety of visual and plastic arts represented in *Mountain Patterns* are the cultural result of life in this physically demanding but visually spectacular environment. As a Nuosu song describes the landscape pattern of the good life,

We come to the mountains behind our house to raise sheep;
The sheep are like massed clouds.
We come to the plains in front of our door to grow grain;

Mountain Patterns brings the visual environment and material culture of Nimu to an international audience. The *Mountain Patterns* exhibit uses architectural elements—walls, doors, hearthstones, pillars, beams, and eaves—specially commissioned from Nuosu artisans to frame the gallery and locate the objects spatially. In the entry hall, the visitor first sees the hearth, with its characteristic three carved stones, and then proceeds through a low wooden doorway to the courtyard, where sets of clothing for female and male, old and young, and married and unmarried Nuosu from different regions of Liangshan are displayed.

Each outfit tells its own story about the home and the social status of its wearer.

Coming back through another low doorway into the interior area, the viewer finds other Nuosu plastic arts: traditional and factory-made lacquerware; ornaments and utensils of pounded silver; a variety of musical instruments, each accompanied by recorded sounds; and a display of the books, paintings, and ritual implements of a Nuosu *bimo*, or priest, the keeper of traditional knowledge in such diverse areas as exorcistic rituals and medicinal plants.

Every type of object featured in *Mountain Patterns* is in use in Liangshan today; even the warrior's armor, no longer worn in battle, still finds a place in funeral rituals. But the society that produces and uses these artifacts is part of the modern world. The *bimo* operates alongside the nurse-practitioner; patchwork skirts and fringed capes on cold days are worn over sneakers and warm-up pants; and a visitor to today's Nimu is as likely to hear boom boxes playing Chinese disco as to pick up the reedy tone of the end-blown flute or the twang of the *hxohxo*, or mouth-harp. Or, perhaps most interestingly, the boom box might be playing tapes of the flute or the *hxohxo*. *Mountain Patterns* is not about a traditional culture frozen in time, cut off from outside influences, "discovered" by some mythically heroic outside adventurer. It is about a cultural renaissance after a dark period of suppression, about uneasy compromises between tradition and modernity, between a local ethnic minority and a modernizing regime, about the survival of Nuosu culture in modern China.

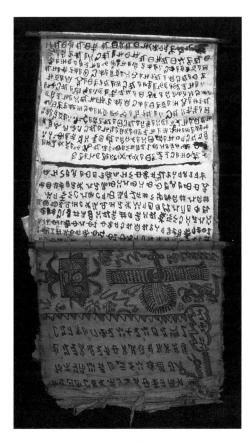

1.4. Hand-copied ritual text

1.5. Bamo Qubumo modeling a 1930s wedding coat in Yynuo style. (Photo by Stevan Harrell)

Traditional Nuosu Society

Until 1956 the Nuosu heartland was never ruled effectively by any outside power, imperial or modern. Westerners called the inhabitants by the Chinese nickname "Lolo" ("Luoluo" in standard Chinese) and thus sometimes referred to the area as "independent Lololand." The Nuosu lived a tribal existence—without permanent rulers, without courts or other formal governmental institutions, without clearly marked territories. Their society was ordered by a complex network of patrilineal clans, each commanding the absolute loyalty of its members, ready to fight to defend themselves against territorial or personal insults from others, but also ready to marry and ally with neighbor clans. Relations between and within clans were governed by elaborate codes of customary law, unwritten but passed down from one generation to the next. Cases in customary law were adjudicated by mediators, called *ndeggu*, whose position was not hereditary or even formal, but who gained respect by being knowledgeable, patient, fair, and articulate.

Clans are tied to one another by marriage. In the old days a young woman and man were matched, often as children, by their parents and their clan elders, and ideally male clan members stayed in one place after marriage while females moved back and forth across the generations. The wedding coat shown here (fig. 1.5) was worn by four generations of mothers and daughters, each moving back to where her mother had come from, until the fourth generation had no daughters, and so they sold the coat. In this way, clans that married each other formed political and sometimes military alliances, but a reneged marriage arrangement or maltreatment of a daughter married out might mean the breach of relations, or even fighting between the clans. Today when Nuosu strangers meet, the first thing they inquire about is clan affiliation. Those in the same clan will recite their paternal genealogies for as many generations as it takes to find the nearest common ancestor. Some aristocrats can recite their genealogies for sixty generations or more, to Gguhxo and Qoni, the legendary founders of the Nuosu, and even commoners ordinarily know twenty generations or so.

Clans were ranked into castes. During various historical periods, Chinese imperial governments appointed *tusi*, or local rulers, from the members of a high-caste Nuosu group know as the *nzymo*, but their rule often lay uneasy on the land, and in recent centuries they lost influence to the aristocratic *nuoho*, who ruled locally without benefit of formal government institutions. The *nuoho* in most places were overlords of the commoner *qunuo*. Both were masters of the *mgajie* (serfs), subject people who worked on the land, and the *gaxy* (slaves), who were personal retainers of the *nuoho* or *qunuo* masters. These *gaxy* were often captured Han or other farmers who got too close or who failed in their obligations to powerful Nuosu.

Where *nuoho* lords and *qunuo* retainers lived together, the retainers owed their overlords labor services; gifts at marriages, funerals, and holidays; and loyalty in war. When the lords moved, as they frequently did in this very mobile society, the retainers often moved with them. In some places, there were no clans representing the aristocratic caste, and so *qunuo* commoners were the effective local lords, ruling over serfs and slaves. The serfs, whether servants of commoners or aristocrats, were bound to the land but carried out their own independent household economies. The slaves labored at the behest of their masters and had no independent economic existence. When slaves were allowed by their masters to marry, they could then set up independent households and in effect could rise to the slightly less debased position of serfs.

Castes preserved their unity and purity by strict prohibitions against marriage between castes. This meant that serfs could almost never rise to the status of commoners, and commoners never crossed the line into the aristocracy. A clan that allowed one of its members to marry someone from a lower caste would be ostracized by its caste peers and thus be unable to contract further marriages, and unfortunate young lovers who tried to cross caste lines would be compelled by customary law to commit suicide as a penalty for their indiscretion. Although they did not inter-marry, members of different castes interacted casually in everyday life. Only on certain occasions would it be possible to tell which people in a community held which rank.

If clan and caste were the warp and woof of the fabric of Nuosu society, there was also a pattern of bright threads represented by people of outstanding ability in different walks of life. Every community had its *suyy* and *suga*, the prominent and the rich, those who achieved preeminence by a combination of ability and strong clan connections. Those distinguished in warfare were known as *ssako*, or brave ones, while *ndeggu* were the wise mediators famed for their impartial settlement of disputes. Religion and ritual were also the province of specialists: *bimo* priests, featured in chapters 7 and 8, were males from specific clans with priestly traditions; interestingly, almost all of the *bimo* clans were commoners. The ambiguity of social status was expressed in the proverb "When the *nzymo* [local ruler, or *tusi*] comes, the *bimo* does not have to stand up out of respect" (Nzy la bi a de). In addition to the *bimo*, there was another kind of religious specialist, the *sunyi*, or shaman, who derived authority from inspiration rather than from book knowledge. Unlike a *bimo*, a *sunyi* could come from any clan or even from the serf or slave strata and could be either a man or a woman.

Craft specialists, too, enjoyed a place of high honor in traditional Nuosu society. The lacquerware, silver ornaments, and musical instruments featured in *Mountain Patterns* are the products of specialist artisans, or *gemo*, whose craft also in many cases passes from generation to generation within the clan. Traditional craft clans also assert their social status in a manner similar to that of *bimo*, saying, "When the *bimo* comes, the craft specialist is not obligated to stand up" (Bi la ge a de).

Most of the artifacts in *Mountain Patterns*, however, are not made by those with any special social, religious, caste, clan, or craft status, but by women who are skilled with spindle and loom, with needle and thread. The status of women in Nuosu society is much like a caste or clan status: fixed at birth and immutable, of course, but subject to individual achievement. An aristocrat remained an aristocrat whether rich or poor, clever or stupid, industrious or lazy, but his reputation depended much more on his accomplishments than on his immutable caste status. So, too, with gender: a woman was destined at birth to wear skirts, to marry into her husband's household, and to take a subordinate position on formal occasions. Taboos prevented her from climbing the ladder to the loft to get potatoes or other stored foods, and she could never, despite her skills or interest, become a *bimo*, which in the traditional society meant that she would almost certainly remain illiterate. But she might still become a master artist, a shaman, even a mediator or warrior. There were thus considerable opportunities for a skilled and ambitious woman to gain respect and reputation. But the most ubiquitous productive accomplishments of Nuosu women were in the area of textiles—weaving, sewing, and embroidery, as so copiously displayed in chapter 3 (fig. 1.6). From shearing to weaving to sewing to appliqué and embroidery, the handiwork of Nuosu women was, and continues to be, as prominent socially as visually. The clothes that a woman manufactured for herself, her children, and her husband were markers of gender, age, marital status, and, most importantly, home town of the wearer. Women's needlework thus expressed, in a visual and visible medium, many elements of the pattern of the Liangshan social fabric.

Nuosu Culture, Chinese Society, and the Modern World

Despite the forbidding topography of their mountain fastness, despite their martial skills and bravery, and despite their absolute prohibition on intermarriage with other ethnic groups, the Nuosu have never lived in complete isolation. They are one of a large number of Yi peoples, related to other ethnic groups in Yunnan and Guizhou who have closely related languages, similar religious systems, and common historical roots. The Yi may have originated as culturally distinct peoples to the north of the Tibetan Plateau, from whence they migrated to Yunnan, or their culture may have developed more or less in situ in Yunnan itself. But from at least the middle of the first millennium B.C.E. until the Mongol conquest of the Dali empire in 1253 C.E., the Yi were a politically prominent, sometimes ruling group in the area of Yunnan, western Guizhou, and southern Sichuan. The Nuosu are, in fact, a minority among the Yi, with a population of around two million, in contrast to the four and a half million among various Yi groups in Yunnan and another million in Guizhou.

Most other Yi groups have truly hybrid cultures. Since they established their own empires (subject to Chinese influence) in the seventh to ninth centuries, and especially since the Mongol conquest in 1253, they have adopted, adapted, and blended many Han Chinese elements with elements taken from the common Yi tradition or developed idiosyncratically in particular localities. Yunnanese Yi, for example, practice religious rites that combine native elements with texts and rituals that are derived from Daoism or other Chinese religions; in some places they even build temples and practice Buddhism. Their languages display large numbers of Chinese loan words; their houses are often indistinguishable from those of Han Chinese, even to the point of being decorated with red couplets over the doors at the New Year; and their family and social organization often show Chinese influences. These hybrid cultures are rich and creative in their own right, but they are not as distinctive, as separate from surrounding cultures, as the unique cultural formations of the Nuosu.

1.6. An expert seamstress hand-sewing a Shynra-style jacket for sale. (Photo by Stevan Harrell)

Exactly when the Yi peoples entered Liangshan is not reliably known, but it is clear that they have been there a thousand years or more and that their society and culture have developed in a unique direction, quite different from the hybrid one taken by their Yi cousins in Yunnan and Guizhou. Even this unique direction is not devoid of outside influence, however. It is very likely that the tribal organization of the Nuosu is not some sort of primitive survival of the time before states formed on the human landscape, but is rather a conscious reaction to the incursions of states upon the Nuosu territory. For example, the last three imperial continental dynasties of East Asia—the Mongol Yuan (1279–1368), the Chinese Ming (1368–1644), and the Manchu Qing (1644–1912)—all ruled their southwestern frontier areas through appointing native rulers, or *tusi*, from the upper strata of the multiple ethnic groups in the area. In Nuosu areas, both the Yuan and the Ming rulers appointed *tusi* from among the preexisting stratum known as *nzymo*; many parts of Liangshan were under *nzymo* rule during these times. But *nzymo* hegemony was never universal in Nimu, and toward the end of the Ming period aristocratic *nuoho* clans in many areas revolted and drove the often highly Hanified *nzymo* away from the Nuosu core areas toward the peripheries of the territory. Thus, in the twentieth century, Liangshan consisted of a patchwork of *nzymo*-ruled areas, areas dominated by aristocratic *nuoho*, and a few places where neither of these upper strata was present and the commoner *qunuo* were the de facto local lords.

An example of a sphere in which there has been Chinese influence on Nuosu culture is the calendar. Nuosu have their own New Year, which comes in late fall, and some of their own holidays. But they use the same twelve animals for the year and month as are used in traditional calendars all over East Asia. In fact, unlike the Chinese, the Nuosu have retained the animal names for the months, and they have inverted the order, so that the year starts with Horse (the seventh animal in the Chinese cycle) in the spring and proceeds from Pig (the last) to Rat (the beginning of a new cycle) in the fall.

Nuosu also depended historically on trade with Chinese areas for certain important goods, such as metal cooking utensils, silver, and gold, and (when they could afford them) various Chinese luxuries. At the end of the nineteenth century this trade was intensified by the introduction of guns and ammunition into Nuosu warfare, and by the ability of Nuosu to produce opium (of which clan elders often strictly prohibited consumption) to trade for guns and for other luxury goods. There is some evidence that as Chinese pressure on the margins increased in the nineteenth and twentieth centuries, Nuosu resistance also stepped up, in the form of more frequent slave raids on Chinese farm settlements on the periphery. In the nineteenth and early twentieth centuries, it was impossible for Chinese or other outsiders to enter the core areas of Nuosu country without an escort supported by leaders of locally powerful clans.

While Chinese pressure on the heartland was increasing, however, Nuosu were also expanding to the west, out of their traditional territory to the east of the Anning River and into the western part of what is now Liangshan Prefecture, an area previously occupied by Qiang-speaking peoples who were ruled by *tusi* of varying ethnicities and were known in Chinese as Xifan, or "Western Barbarians." By the early twentieth century, Nuosu clans had taken over many parts of this Western area politically and demographically, but nowhere in the western area is there a solid core of Nuosu relatively uninfluenced by the outside, as there is in the eastern core area. This means that there have been many reciprocal cultural influences between Nuosu and local Han Chinese in this area, but there have been more with the native Xifan peoples, from whom the Nuosu have adopted such customs as raising yaks and drinking butter tea, something unknown in the Nuosu heartland.

Despite this long history of contact and some mutual influence with neighboring peoples, however, no outside influence on Nuosu society and culture up to the mid-twentieth century was anywhere near as profound or as threatening as the changes wrought by the Chinese Communist Party after its army occupied the area in 1950. At the beginning of their administration, the Communists assumed control and set up some administrative units, but they did not radically alter the Nuosu social structure. They did, however, make an important designation: they classified the Nuosu, along with most of the other peoples of Yunnan and Guizhou previously known as "Luoluo," as members of the Yi *minzu* (nationality, ethnic group). To this day, the Nuosu are known in Chinese as the Yi of Liangshan.

Beginning in 1956 the Communists instituted what they called the "Democratic Reforms." This was a comprehensive effort to abolish what they saw as the exploitative and oppressive aspects of what they termed the "slave society" in Liangshan, and to set the Nuosu, along with the rest of the citizens of China, on the road to socialist modernization. The first task was the abolition of slavery and serfdom, which was quickly followed by the institution of collective farming in the early 1960s. At the same time, county governments were established in the heart of Nuosu territory, where they had not existed before, and schools were begun, both to teach ordinary people to be literate in Chinese (and to a limited extent in a romanized form of Nuosu) and to train Nuosu for cadre, teaching, and technical positions in the Chinese bureaucracy. This also meant building roads where there were nothing but trails; cities where there had been only occasional markets or small-town trading posts; and schools, offices, and other public buildings where there had been only private residences and the occasional fortified government outpost. At the early stages of the reforms, however, Party workers took special care to cooperate with local elites and to carry out the proposed social changes in a nonantagonistic way. This was very different from the bloody land-reform struggles that had seized most of China a few years earlier.

These early reforms by themselves were opposed only by a small portion of conservatives among the Nuosu elite; others had realized for decades that they would have to enter the modern world at some stage and sought ways to do this on their own terms. But in the late 1950s the Chinese government turned radical, implementing nationwide such extreme social reforms as the Great Leap Forward and the People's Communes. Liangshan was no exception to these policies, which also involved the abandonment of gentler, more cooperative methods for the fire of class struggle. This soon prompted an aristocrat-led revolt that lasted several years and divided some Nuosu clans and families into those who fought for the rebels and those who fought on the government side.

The revolt never had much chance of success and was put down within a year or two in most areas. But it was not long after the end of the revolt and the recovery from the nationwide famine of 1959–61 that the Great Proletarian Cultural Revolution seized Liangshan as it seized the rest of China. More than any event in history, the Cultural Revolution of 1966–76 threatened the survival of Nuosu culture. Schools no longer taught the Nuosu language in any form, but adopted the policy of "direct transition" to Chinese-language education. *Bimo*, the repositories of so much traditional ritual and naturalistic knowledge, were labeled "feudal superstitious practitioners" and forbidden to perform rituals, read and copy texts, or teach their sons and nephews as disciples. Any activities by clans acting in concert were immediately put down as "counterrevolutionary," and government cadres became the only legitimate authorities. Nuosu culture was far from being totally obliterated during this time: of course it was impractical to force everyone to speak Chinese, which most Nuosu did not know at all; as long as women sewed their own clothes, they would sew skirts and not slacks; and some *bimo* even managed to conduct the most important rituals secretly in attenuated form. But the Cultural Revolution set up an adversarial relationship between traditional culture and state authority, between local practice and modern development. It put the Nuosu on a path that would eventually have led to cultural amalgamation and the loss of most or all of the heritage that we see in *Mountain Patterns*.

But the Communist Party in the early 1980s explicitly repudiated the Cultural Revolution and its radical policies toward ethnic minority integration at the same time that it proclaimed modernization and economic development as the most important goals for the nation. This presented a paradox for the Nuosu. On the one hand, they were free again to exercise many cultural elements. They developed a modified version of the traditional writing system, which is now taught in schools all over Nuosu country and is also used for scholarly and popular books, as well as a daily newspaper and a few magazines. They encouraged redevelopment of arts and crafts of all kinds, building factories to mass-produce lacquerware and making available the brightly colored synthetic fabrics and yarns used in much modern clothing. They resumed collation and editing of traditional texts and the study of traditional musical forms. Perhaps most significantly, they succeeded in changing the status of the *bimo* from "feudal superstitious practitioners"

to "ethnic intellectuals," thus opening the door first for study of their texts and then, in the 1990s, to full-blown ritual activity for them and for *sunyi* as well. In many ways, the last fifteen years have been a golden age of revival and innovation in Nuosu cultural forms of all sorts.

At the same time, however, there is another threat— modern consumer culture has come to Nimu in great force, especially since 1990. The market at Niuniuba in Meigu, for example, one of the largest traditional marketplaces in Nuosu territory, now sells many times more cheap blouses and slacks than it sells skirts and embroidery threads. Women in many parts of Liangshan now wear skirts only for dress-up occasions such as weddings and holidays. Disco and even Chinese rock are heard alongside folk music. But at present, we should be careful about sounding any alarms of ruin. Affordable clothes that do not take hours of work to make—and are easy to wash—are not a bad thing in themselves, nor is contemporary music. There are, after all, even Nuosu rock groups; one of them has made three tapes, with some songs in Nuosu and some in Chinese. And there are still places where the tendency to revive cultural forms after the repression of the revolution outweighs that to jettison them in favor of global pop culture. Young men still learn to sing the traditional "praise songs" of their clans, and almost as many boys in Meigu County are studying to become *bimo* as are in regular schools, whatever the result may be for economic development. The challenge now for Nuosu who have some knowledge of the wider world (and they are still a minority) is to manage wisely the tension between cultural survival and economic development. It would be a great loss for the Nuosu if development passed them by, for Nimu is still a poor, unhealthy, and often brutal environment, despite its natural and cultural beauty. It would be an equally great loss for the Nuosu and for the world if development and consumer culture finally smeared out the exquisite mountain patterns that have survived the efforts of so many regimes to tame them and have regenerated themselves so spectacularly after the dark years of the Cultural Revolution. For now, *Mountain Patterns* introduces these arts to the world at a time when they are still very much alive.

CHAPTER 2

Nuosu Architecture

BAMO QUBUMO

Nuosu villages and houses have a strong flavor of the montane forest. From the layout of villages to the selection of house sites, from the shape and structure of houses to the arrangement of villages, from the spatial relationships among rooms to the beliefs and taboos surrounding their use, everything in Nuosu architecture exhibits the heritage of a unique mode of mountain living.

The Concentration and Scattering of Natural Villages

Most Nuosu live in mountainous and foothill areas at elevations between six thousand and ten thousand feet, and villages sites can be selected on steep, high mountain slopes (fig. 2.1) or warmer plains or in valleys formed by mountain streams. A place up against the mountains and next

2.1. Yangjuan, Ma Erzi's home village. (Photo by Stevan Harrell)

to the streams, where they can herd sheep in the meadows, hunt game in the forests, and grow grain on the gentle slopes or the alluvial plains, is the ideal village site for the Nuosu. This is the type of residence described in the epic *Book of Creation* (Hnewo Teyy) for the ancestral land of Zyzypuvu:

In back of the house are mountains, where we can herd our
   sheep;
In front of the house are plains, where we can grow our grain;
On the plains there is a field, where we can race horses;
The wetlands are ideal for raising pigs;

In the village there is a place for the children to play;
In the house there is a place for the women to sit;
In front of the door there is a place to entertain guests.

Nuosu villages are not large; many have just three to five houses, though some have as many as a hundred. In general, houses are more scattered in the mountains and more concentrated into villages on the alluvial plains. Nuosu in Liangshan often choose high places or steep topography for their houses. Dwellings are scattered below overhanging cliffs, in inaccessible forests, and on forbidding slopes amidst the mountains, and one sees roofs in green, steep-sided valleys and on the slopes above. In the Anning Valley, people customarily gather a whole clan into a single village, with houses clustered closely together amid layer upon layer of rice fields.

House Sites

Nuosu are very particular about where they build their houses. Traditional processes are used to select a site and divine the fate of a house.

SELECTING THE SITE

Nuosu beliefs about where to build houses differ slightly from region to region. In general, the ideal place to build is where "in back of the house are high mountains, high mountains for herding cattle and sheep, and in front of the house is a plain, a plain for growing the five grains." Thus there are many taboos concerning site selection: a house facing a barren mountain is inauspicious and will bring poverty; one facing a mountain with luxuriant trees and undergrowth will bring prosperity; and a stream in front of the house is greatly auspicious, while one in back is forbidden and will bring mountain floods that endanger the house (fig. 1.3). In areas where Nuosu live mixed with Han, they have absorbed Han ideas of *fengshui* (geomancy) and when selecting a house site give careful thought to the "dragon veins" in the earth.

DIVINING THE FATE OF THE HOUSE

After selecting the site, one must perform a divination to determine whether it is auspicious or inauspicious. Usually people ask a *bimo* and prominent elders to do the divination. Nuosu not only try to correlate the horoscopes of the male and female heads of household, but they also use several methods of divination to determine whether their stay there will be fortunate or unfortunate. In the Yynuo, or northern Nuosu, area there are three primary methods:

rolling an egg, rice-grain divination, and burning a sheep scapula.

Rolling an Egg (Vaqi Mbie). The household head takes an egg and rolls it on the selected site. After this, three stones are set up in a hearth arrangement with an iron wok on top, in which the egg is boiled. The boiled egg is taken out and shelled, and if the yolk is straight and not crooked, this is a good sign; if not, another site must be selected.

Rice-Grain Divination (Chequ Mbie). The household head takes five grains of rice in his hand and quickly sticks them in the ground, one at each of the four compass points and one in the middle, and then uses a bowl to pound them into place. The next day he inspects them, and if any are gone or have fallen over, this is inauspicious and another site must be chosen.

Burning a Sheep Scapula (Yopy Jy). This requires the services of a *bimo*, who, after burning some straw on a sheep scapula, examines the charred patterns. A square is the most auspicious; a straight line is middling; and criss-crossing lines are inauspicious.

Housebuilding Rituals

Building a house is a major event. The major stages in the building process are laying the foundation, raising the beams, setting the doorway, putting up the corner posts, shingling the roof, and constructing the hearth. For each of these stages, one must ask a *munyisico* (horoscopist) or a *bimo* to choose an auspicious day that coordinates with the birth year of the female head of household. Each stage in the process is also accompanied by the appropriate ritual, most importantly those for groundbreaking, raising the beams, moving into the house, and constructing the hearth.

GROUNDBREAKING (*ZZAXI NDU*)

Groundbreaking must be done in a year when the mistress is an odd-numbered age, and the direction in which the front door faces must harmonize with her horoscope. Though most doors face east and downhill, one may not locate them thus if doing so would conflict with the mistress's horoscope. If the day of groundbreaking is not particularly auspicious, one must dig out a little soil a few days before and put it in the current house. On the day of groundbreaking, the master must wine and dine relatives and friends. If the first earth dug is found to contain water, ashes, or bones, which are inauspicious, a different site must be selected.

RAISING THE BEAM (YISI ZZI)

The owner who is building the house first cuts a little slot in the beam and inserts some silver coins to promote wealth, and then ties a red cloth on it to demonstrate the skill of the carpenter. After the beam is in place, a red rooster is put on it, facing the rear of the house. If the rooster jumps down facing the door, this is auspicious; if not, it is inauspicious and the construction process will not proceed smoothly, so the master must have a ritual performed to expel any ghosts or inauspicious influences.

MOVING IN (YI VUR)

After the house is built, the first thing the owners must do is hang an eagle's claw, ox horns, and ram's horns over the doorway to pacify the household and keep out evil. Before the owners move in, two people, each carrying a mulberry branch, should walk through the house, one to the right and one to the left, spitting liquor on the walls as they go, murmuring a verse whose meaning is "All the bones and ashes who came into the house when the earth was being dug and pounded into walls, all the ghosts and demons who came in with the lumber and shingles, get out!" Afterward, as they exit through the doorway, they should stick the mulberry branches above the door to demonstrate that the evil influences are gone. Then an ox is driven into the house, and the wine-spitters yell, "Good luck, come! Riches, roll in! Bearers of roasted flour, bearers of firewood, hundreds, thousands, ten thousands of sons and grandsons!" Then the mistress, the master, and the children enter the house. It is taboo for the master to go in front, for that would prevent the household from prospering. Then fire is built with tongs, demonstrating the beginning of the "fire and smoke" of the household. On this day the family cannot eat steamed rice. If they did so, their "bones would be nibbled"—they would be poor. Instead, this day they may eat only rice gruel, brought by neighbors to congratulate them on moving in.

BUILDING THE HEARTH

Digging the hearth-pit and erecting the hearthstones are two different processes, but they can be carried out on the same day. An auspicious day must be selected; otherwise all the livestock would die. The earth dug out to form the hearth-pit cannot be taken outside the house, where the stars could see it, for this would be inauspicious.

People take considerable care in selecting the hearth-stones for their homes. Most important, stones must be clean—they may not be from near a cremation ground or have bird or animal excrement on them. Either natural stones or stones cut by artisans—often with designs of mythical birds and animals, or with floral or other patterns—may be used. The three hearthstones face inward, but the stone representing the master and that representing the mistress should be turned a little more toward each other, while the guest stone should be turned a little to the side; this represents the common aspirations of the household members.

2.2. Roof made of cedar shingles, held in place by rocks

Shingle-Roofed Houses

When you walk into a Nuosu village, the first thing you will notice is the array of archaic-looking shingle-roofed houses. Only if you take a closer look, though, will you be able to appreciate their particular architectural genius. Nuosu call them *piyi*, which means "board houses," because their steep, peaked roofs are made of cedar shingles, which are used like tiles (fig. 2.2). Their plans may be

2.3. Beams and rafters of an elaborate house

Still, the construction genius of the shingled houses is difficult to see from a distance. You have to enter the house and wait until your eyes have adjusted to the dim and flickering light of pine resin or of the wood and grass burning in the hearth to discern its details.

The span of the interior walls relies on post-and-beam construction to bear the weight, and the walls are filled in with tamped earth and planks. The interlocking horizontal crosspieces and vertical suspended timbers, which do not reach the ground, all form a network of perpendicular and proportional parts that is nevertheless particularly suited to creative adaptation (fig. 2.3). Between roof beams and between posts are decorative wooden struts of various lengths that are jointed together; this gives the overall effect in the upper spaces of the house of the mutual construction of full and empty spaces. The struts of various sizes attach to each other in a series of ascending levels, and the little suspended posts of various lengths hang down, sometimes by the hundreds. The lower ends of these suspended posts, whether carved as ox heads or sheep heads, express a feeling of aus-

rectangular, or they may be built as three- or four-sided houses around a courtyard, and their walls may be of mud or bamboo. The shingles look simple, but in fact they incorporate skilled workmanship. The flat shingles, about 1.5 by 0.5 meters in size, are split with a knife, rather than sawed. In nearby forests, Nuosu select timber of the right thickness that is straight-grained and free of knots. After felling, trees are cut into sections of appropriate length and then split into straight-grained, sturdy shingles. The shingles are placed in two layers on top of the structural beams and rafters, with the second layer laid over the gaps between the shingles in the first, and the whole thing held down by

2.4. Front door of a house with overhanging eaves decorated with ox-head patterns.
(Photo by Bamo Qubumo)

stones placed on top. Because the natural vertical grain of the shingles forms small grooves, rainwater and snow will flow downward with the grain and will not ruin the roof. Some such roofs last for three generations or up to a hundred years.

piciousness and good fortune (fig. 2.4). All interior walls are made of wooden planks, often carved in traditional patterns with exquisite artistic skill. Interior divisions of rooms also often use jointed wooden boards closely fitted together for an aesthetically pleasing effect. Some shingled houses also have a posted verandah and/or overhanging eaves, and the decorative struts penetrate the walls to form part of these copious exterior eave decorations (figs. 2.5–6; pls. 3–4).

In decorating houses, Nuosu artisans use a series of carved and painted patterns inherited for many generations. Visually the decorations are concentrated around the main doorway and in the eaves. The doorway is often given an arched form, and on the lintel are carved patterns of sun and moon, birds and animals. Soffits can be carved in sawtooth patterns or simple designs; the middle portion and the two ends of the ridgepole may be arched or upswept. Carvings of ox heads, goat heads (to anchor the house), sheep heads (to bring good fortune), wild birds and animals, or other chaining, repeated patterns appear on the end eaves, arched doorways, suspended vertical timbers, and horizontal crosspieces. On interior walls and partitions are even and symmetrical patterns of buds, flowers, plants, and animals (pl. 2). In some houses the wood is preserved in its natural color; in others lacquer is added for a rich architectural effect.

The extensive knowledge of Nuosu carpenters is expressed in house construction without the use of rulers, nails, or blueprints. The whole design and the detailed plans are all in their heads, put together with mind and hand. Yet the fit between the posts, beams, rafters, crosspieces, and vertical timbers is exact, so close that it gives extraordinary strength to the houses. The shingled house is the focal point of Nuosu architecture, the crystallization of the knowledge and skill of the carpenter, a poetic expression of the adaptation of life to the forested mountain environment. This type of Nuosu house has been praised by Chinese architectural scholars as a marvel of China's folk architecture.

Watchtowers, Guardsmen of the Village

Historically, clan feuds and blood vendettas between clans rose and fell over the ages, and the imperial troops of the dynasties whose territory ringed Liangshan often attacked. In order to keep watch and to defend against attacks and invasions, the *nuoho* aristocrats in many areas built watchtowers next to their courtyards. Watchtowers had wood frames and mud walls, sometimes reinforced with granite (fig. 2.7). The lowest were two stories, and the highest as many as nine, with high, thick walls on all four sides. Their defensive preparations were thorough, and they had gun ports, arrow ports, and observation terraces. Backed up against high mountains, they were steadfast, for, looking

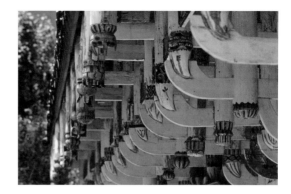

2.5. Repeated eave decorations

2.6. Detail of an ox-head eave decoration

2.7. Watchtower

down from heights, they were easy to defend and difficult to attack. An imposing watchtower on the ridges or the mountain slopes was like a brave warrior, defending the Nuosu village. This kind of traditional military construction is still preserved in the construction of Nuosu houses, although its function has changed. Viewed from afar, tall and short watchtowers sitting in the shadow of the tall trees still impart a particularly Nuosu architectural pattern to the mountain villages.

The Floor Hearth, Sacred Place within the House

The hearth is the center of activity for every Nuosu household (fig. 2.8)—the place for eating, drinking, getting warm, finding light, entertaining guests, and discussing affairs, and even for religious activities. Nuosu view the hearth as the symbol of the household, connecting it closely to the fortunes of the household members. There is a close connection between the fates of the household members and the lighting and extinguishing of the fire. For this reason, the "ten-thousand-year fire" must never be completely extinguished while people live in a house.

Usually the hearth is situated behind the front door to the main room of the house, on either the right or left, depending on the direction in which the door opens. The pit of the hearth is usually round, sometimes hexagonal. Usually there is a foundation of stone within the earth, in which are inserted three hearthstones called *galy* (fig. 2.9), forming a three-stoned tripod. Places around the hearth are divided into hosts' places (*nyimu*), guests' places (*galo*), and lower places (*gajy*). When guests come, they and the hosts usually sit around the fire, but they pay great attention to precedence in sitting, which is usually in order from eldest to youngest.

2.9. Detail of an incised hearthstone

In some houses there is an ancestral altar above the hearth, the most sacred and forbidden place in the household. When worshipping the ancestors, one must first perform a purifying ritual of heating a stone and quenching it in water. When making offerings, the offerings should first be raised above the hearth to demonstrate that they have been purified. When households perform domestic sacrifices or rituals inside the house, they do them next to the hearth. For example, when calling a lost soul, one must first call the soul to return to the hearthside, so that the soul may return to the body. When a bride leaves her natal family, she must be carried around the hearth three times by one of her relatives, to represent the parting of the bride and her family. There are many taboos regarding the hearth, such as not stepping on it, not jumping over it, and not spitting water into it. The perpetual fire in the hearth reflects Nuosu reverence for fire.

[Translated by Stevan Harrell]

2.8. A family entertaining guests while preparing a meal on the hearth. (Photo by Stevan Harrell)

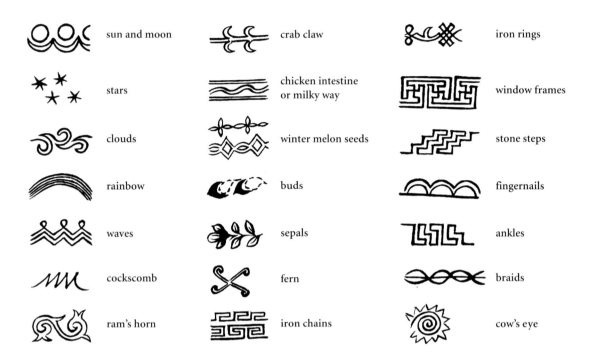

sun and moon	crab claw	iron rings
stars	chicken intestine or milky way	window frames
clouds	winter melon seeds	stone steps
rainbow	buds	fingernails
waves	sepals	ankles
cockscomb	fern	braids
ram's horn	iron chains	cow's eye

3.1. Patterns employed in Nuosu textiles and lacquerware. (Adapted from Liangshan Zhou Bowuguan, *Niepsha Nuosu Shibbop Lotwa Bburyi Dafut: Vitgga* [Chengdu: Sichuan Minzu Chubanshe, 1985])

Clothing and Textiles

BAMO QUBUMO

3.2. Shynra "medium pant legs," smaller than "big pant legs" but still loose

3.3. Suondi "small pant legs," fitting almost snugly around the ankles

THE BASIC PRINCIPLES OF TRADITIONAL NUOSU CLOTHING are simple—males wear pants and put their hair up, females wear full, pleated skirts and cloth headdresses, and both sexes of all ages wear felt capes or woven, fringed capes—yet each local area has its own materials, patterns, accessories, and decorative motifs. It is customary to divide the Nuosu into three dialect areas, and clothing is similarly classified according to the width of the men's trouser legs: the Yynuo style in northern Liangshan features "big trouser legs"; Shynra, in central Liangshan, "medium trouser legs"; and Suondi, in the south, "small trouser legs." These three regional styles differ in shape, pattern, weave, color, and techniques of manufacture (pl. 5; figs. 3.2–3).

The materials used to make Nuosu clothing have changed throughout the ages. The most important materials have been woven hemp, woven wool, wool felt, tanned leather, straw and bamboo matting, cotton, and silk. Today fabric woven of mixed wool and hemp has just about disappeared, being confined to women's sanitary products. Things still made from traditional materials include pleated and fringed wool capes (*jieshy* and *vala*), sheepskin cloaks, straw rain capes, straw sandals, felt boots, and deerskin satchels.

Spinning and Weaving

Spinning and weaving are household tasks ordinarily undertaken by women and form an important part of their lives. Skill in these arts is an important standard for judging the worth of a woman. The long narrative poem "Mother's Daughter" movingly describes the scene of spinning and weaving:

The black cape takes nine widths of cloth;
The pleated skirt has very fine weave.
Daughter holds wool in her left hand;
It looks exactly like white clouds.
Daughter lifts the spun thread in her right hand;
The spindle turns without stopping;
The spun yarn stretches out straight.
She spins with the speed of the arrow leaving the bowstring;
The yarn coils flash like splashing hail.

The most important material for spinning and weaving is sheep's wool. In the past, women also spun small amounts of thread out of hemp and out of wild nettles.

WOOLEN CLOTH

Nuosu can shear and store wool only during the yearly shearing season. When they weave, they either spread it out and tear it very fine or use a bamboo bow to beat it to a downy consistency, rather like cotton wadding, and place it in a little spinning basket woven of bamboo skin. They then use a special spindle to spin it into fine woolen yarn (pl. 6). Two or three strands are twisted into a thread, which is woven into woolen cloth.

WEAVING TECHNIQUE

The weaver finds a flat place inside the house or outdoors and drives a wooden peg about as thick as the bottom of a rice bowl into the ground. She ties one end of the warp

3.4. Weaving wool for a *vala*, front view. (Photo by Stevan Harrell)

yarn to the peg and the other to the loom, which is held in front of her body, anchored by a wide back-strap. She passes the woof yarn with the shuttle back and forth from left to right with both hands, and after each pass pulls hard with the wooden batten to pack the woof tightly (figs. 3.4–5).

Nuosu women produce cloth in both a plain weave and a twill weave. Home-woven woolen cloth is used primarily for skirts and *vala*.

HEMPEN CLOTH

Nuosu classify hemp into male and female, according to whether it produces flowers and seeds; this is an example of the "gendered world" of the Yi peoples. Usually, the male hemp is harvested first with a knife; then a wooden club is used to thresh it. The fibers are peeled away, and it is rolled into thread with two fibers to a strand. This is boiled in a wok for ten to twelve hours, during which time wood ash is added and the mixture stirred; this makes the cloth tougher and more pliable. Then it is taken to the stream and pound-washed, after which it is soaked in oatmeal

gruel for about an hour, which bleaches it. This hempen yarn can then be woven into cloth, using basically the same techniques used for wool. It is tough and durable, and was previously used to make skirts and feminine hygiene products.

Felting

Felting is a process requiring considerable skill, and one that is undertaken by males. But not every man knows how to do it, so a family that needs felt products will hire

3.5. Weaving wool for a *vala*, back view. (Photo by Stevan Harrell)

a known felter. There are two kinds of felt capes: the unpleated, thick kind known as *vobo* and the vertically pleated, thinner kind known as *jieshy*. The *vobo* can be worn any time, and the quality of the wool is not too important; the *jieshy* is a kind of dress clothing worn for gatherings or when visiting.

Traditional felting tools include the fluffing bow, the bamboo-strip mat, and the rolling mat. On a windless, auspicious day, wool is first ripped apart and then spread out on the bamboo-strip mat, according to the desired size, shape, and thickness, where it is beaten into wadding with the fluffing bow. It is then evened out and sprinkled with a little hot water (fig. 3.6), and the mat is rolled up into a cylinder. Two bamboo poles are inserted in the middle and pulled by two people in opposite directions. When it is pulled tight, three muscular young men stand each with one foot on the ground and the other foot on the bamboo mat cylinder, rolling it back and forth, pressing the wool inside the mat and making it compress into felt. Then a woolen string is put through the collar as a drawstring, and the mat is rolled up and the cylinder rolled back and forth

3.7. Pressing felt into pleats to make a *jieshy*. (Photo by Bamo Qubumo)

with the feet once again. After it is rinsed and dried in the sun, the *vobo* is complete.

When a *jieshy* is rolled, after the felt is taken out of the rolled cylinder it is folded every three fingers' width, pressed between two boards, tied up securely, and stored vertically to allow the water to drain out (fig. 3.7). After ten days or so, it is dry, and when the press is opened, the cape is complete.

Dyeing

Nuosu dyeing appears to use very ancient methods. The dyes, made from infusions of wild plants, produce only black, blue, and red. Black is made by boiling together horse mulberry and lacquer tree bark and leaves, and the filtered liquid is used to soak or steep the textiles, which are then rinsed in river water. The color is permanent and fast. Blue is made with tender shoots and leaves of the *kajji* tree, which are sun-dried and ground into a powder, which is rolled into cakes that are broken into pieces and added to water with leaves of the lacquer tree. Cloth is boiled in this

mixture, and the resulting color is very fast. Red is made from leaves of the walnut tree and powdered roots of the *vu* plant. Textiles are boiled in this mixture two or three times.

Women's Decorative Textile Skills

The beauty and attraction of Nuosu clothing and adornment is all in the skilled and clever hands of Nuosu women. Girls learn from childhood the arts of weaving, sewing, and needlework from their mothers and other village women, and whoever has the best designed outfit or the most outstanding embroidery patterns will receive general praise as well as the attentions of young men. Many women know several different arts and many different patterns. Gems that dazzle the eye include flying birds and running beasts, blowing clouds and running water, mountain flowers and wild grasses—every kind of natural wonder and scenic beauty—all concentrated in the arts of needlecraft and decoration. Both men's and women's clothing is decorated on front panels, across the back, and on the sleeves. There are many different kinds of decoration.

COUCHING

Multicolored threads are braided, or cotton cloth cut into very thin strips, and then bent into patterns such as windows, stairways, chains, waves, and pumpkins and sewn onto the backing cloth (pl. 7).

APPLIQUE

Colored cloth is cut into repeating or duplicate patterns and sewn onto areas of a garment. Borders and corners are outlined with colored thread or cloth strips, which are also used to embroider or cross-stitch around seams. Silver plates and balls can be used for decoration. Patterns include ram's horn, firelighter, and waves (pl. 8).

INSETS

Strips of colored cloth or lengths of embroidery thread are inset on the front panel of a jacket or inserted into a border. A cockscomb pattern is usually used.

EDGING

Colored cloth is used to edge the borders of garments, to bring out the colors more vividly by means of the uneven surface.

EMBROIDERY

Colored silk thread is used to embroider patterns such as flowers, grasses, and leaves. This is very fine work, used most commonly on headcloths and sleeves.

CROSS-STITCHING

Colored silk thread is used to cross-stitch many kinds of neat and intricate patterns. This technique is used mostly on collars and headcloths (pl. 9).

Perhaps the finest examples of Nuosu needlework come from the Yynuo area, where the most common technique is couching, although appliqué and embroidery also are used. A single jacket can use as many as nine colors and patterns. The patterns are neat and elaborate but not chaotic. Colors are vivid and do not fall into any accustomed pattern; the needlework skill is very fine, the patterns carefully thought out (pl. 7).

The Shynra area is characterized by several duplicated continuous patterns made evenly around the hems of all parts of a jacket. These are made with many different decorative techniques. Sometimes there are different patterns on the front panel and across the yoke (pl. 10). The most commonly used patterns are cockscomb, window, and fire-

lighter. Large fern patterns on the shirttail are a unique style, adding up to a coordinated overall pattern.

The clothes of the Suondi area are simple and colorful, with the entire outfit coordinated, using mostly appliqué along with couching and inset techniques. Suondi women like to use strongly contrasting shades of red, yellow, green, blue, and white. They do not pay particular attention to intricacy and skill, so most of their patterns are variations on the ram's horn and firelighter patterns (pl. 8).

The "Sacred Hair" and the "Hero's Horn"

The traditional hairstyle of Nuosu men of all ages featured a little hair left growing on the top of the head, the *nzuolyr*, with the rest shaved. In Nuosu thinking, the *nzuolyr* is a sacred place that should not be violated. Aside from a man's parents and other senior relatives, other people—especially women, children, and (in the past) people of lower caste—cannot touch it.

The form and shape of the *nzuolyr* differ from place to place and according to age and social status. For example, some boys in the Yynuo area have two tufts of hair left at each side of the front of the head like a goat's horns; old people say this protects against ghosts. Some young men twist these two tufts into hanging "goathorn braids." Men in Ganluo sometimes put a piece of bamboo or other stiff material in their hair to make it stand on end. In the Suondi area, some men let their *nzuolyr* grow naturally into a puffy form (figs. 3.8–10).

The "hero's horn," which has been noted in Chinese-language historical texts for over two thousand years, is made by tying the end of a turban into a pointed shape that sticks out in front of the head, and varies according to region and age. Both young and old men pay particular attention to the appearance of this "horn" (figs. 3.11–12).

Jieshy and *Vala*: Clothing by Day, a Raincoat in a Storm, a Cover by Night

The felt cape (*jieshy*) and the woven cape (*vala*) are uniquely Nuosu articles of clothing, worn by both sexes and all ages. Worn together, these two layers provide warmth in winter weather.

Jieshy are of two styles: the single is about two meters wide, with about thirty pleats (fig. 3.13); the double can be as wide as five to six meters, with as many as ninety pleats. The *vala*, a development of the *jieshy*, is made in the twill pattern with home-woven wool, several widths of which are sewn together. *Vala* vary regionally. In the Yynuo area they

3.8. Yynuo boy. (Photo by Bamo Qubumo)

3.9. Goathorn braids. (Photo by Bamo Qubumo)

3.10. Ganluo gathered topknot style

3.11. The prominent *bimo* Qubi Shomo, showing an old Yynuo man's style of "horn." (Photo by Bamo Qubumo)

3.12. A Shynra style of wearing the "horn"

3.13. A bride wearing a *jieshy* waits to enter her husband's house. (Photo by Stevan Harrell)

3.14. Boys wearing unfringed, Yynuo-style *vala*

3.15. Ma Erzi wearing a Shynra-style *vala*. (Photo by Stevan Harrell)

are usually made of undyed wool, fringed or unfringed at the bottom but decorated with one wide and one narrow strip of blue or black cloth along the front edges (fig. 3.14). In the Shynra area they are usually dyed black or blue, with a long fringe along the bottom, and black cloth across the shoulders and the bottom, on which are embroidered fern or wave patterns (fig. 3.15). Suondi *vala* are usually deep blue, just long enough to cover the backside, and with fringe thirty centimeters long. On the top and bottom are red or yellow rickrack borders.

Jieshy and *vala* are not only decorative, but multifunctional. In addition to wearing them as insulation against cold and protection against rain, and using them as covers while sleeping, one can pull the collar drawstring tight and make them into a bag for carrying grain, or fold them up to make a cushion to sit on when out traveling, or women can use them to carry babies, so people have them handy all year long. They are also the formal clothing of the Nuosu, worn on major ritual occasions to emphasize the gravity of the occasion.

The short felt jackets worn by Nuosu men and women are also somewhat unusual. They usually have a cloth lining inside the felt, do not button in front, and fit rather closely. They are very sturdy and often are worn by those working in the fields. Women's short felt jackets often have appliqué

and decorative borders employing bold patterns around the hem and shoulders. Suondi have a distinctive style of short felt jacket, often made of undyed wool or wool dyed dark blue, with two short sleeves; young ladies wearing these vests out walking leisurely look quite elegant (pl. 11).

Sheepskin Overcoats and Straw Raincoats

Yi peoples have worn sheepskin overcoats since ancient times, and today in Liangshan, sheepskin coats are found everywhere. In the Suondi area, a special kind of goatskin coat is also found. Sheepskin coats require five whole skins of the same color, sewn together with the wooly side out. A good sheepskin overcoat takes as long as three years to make. One has to choose five lambs of similar size with similar wool and raise them three years without shearing the wool near the tail, while shearing the rest of the animal three times a year. The length of the skin from shoulder to tail-base is the length of the coat. The unsheared wool should be about thirteen centimeters long, and the sheared portion about three centimeters. The finished coat has a thirty-centimeter strip of thirteen-centimeter-long wool around the hem, with the upper part all short wool. Usually these coats are made of plain black sheepskins, which reflect light and give a dashing appearance. They are heavy and expensive, and owners usually reserve them as treasures to impress people at important gatherings.

Most rain capes are made of woven palm fiber or *yyryyr* mountain grass, both of which are effective against rain and wind (fig. 3.16). Capes made of very pretty horsetail and horse's mane are highly prized.

Children's Clothing

The most striking items of Nuosu children's clothing are their hats. These are similar everywhere, with minor variations, and tend to have designs built around the fern pattern, which has rich symbolic connotations in Nuosu folklore. The fern, which is one of the first plants to grow in spring, whose spores are innumerable, and whose offspring grow close by, symbolizes the proliferation and unity of descendants within the clan and is celebrated in legends, personal names, and place names. In sewing the fern pattern on her child's hat, the mother makes every stitch and every thread reflect her wishes for the health and prosperity of her child.

3.16. Straw raincoat

3.17. Girls' skirts

Children's hats (pls. 12–13; back cover) are the same for girls and for boys, and are all multilayered. An eagle feather is placed in the crown to fend off evil influences, a little bag of musk is hung on the hat to repel illness, and a bullet made of colored thread is hung in order to expel ghosts. Yynuo children's hats have a wave pattern around the edges and a little fringe on the back, so that viewed from the side they look a bit like a rooster, with a comb in front, an arched top, and wings in back. Ganluo children's hats look like small round helmets, with a little brightly colored fringed spear in the middle, resembling the "hero's horn" of male adults. On the

sides of the hat are appliquéd two cute, playful monkeys.

Nuosu boys' clothing is basically the same as the men's, except for the twelve-centimeter red band that boys under ten in the Yynuo area wear around their trouser legs. But girls' clothing is a style of its own, with obvious differences from women's in both head coverings and skirts; one can tell at a glance whether a female Nuosu is considered an adult. Adolescent girls braid their hair into a single braid at the back of the head and wear a single-layered headcloth and a red headband or one with silver plates sewn onto it. Their earrings might feature seashells, deer's teeth, or two or three little red beads; when not wearing earrings, they may keep their ear-piercings open with thread. Their jackets are the same as those of adult women, but often somewhat less decorated. A girls' skirt, or *shahla*, has two layers: the top is cylindrical and usually red or blue, and the bottom pleated and mostly white. Some girls either hang three rows of silk thread, red on the outside and green in the middle, at the places where the two panels of the skirt meet or weave in two stripes of fine colored thread in the top panel, to indicate their childhood state. They also sew dark-colored strips of cloth on the sides of their skirts, as do grown women (fig. 3.17).

CHANGING TO ADULT CLOTHING

When Nuosu girls are between fifteen and seventeen years old, they go through a ceremony called *shahla ge*, "changing the skirt," which marks their passage from girlhood to womanhood. Before the ceremony, they are girls. Whether they have been engaged or not—which is a matter of clan politics—they are still considered innocents, neither sexual nor reproductive. After the ceremony they are adult women who may go out to market, have sweethearts, and take on adult sexual and reproductive roles. The ceremony may be attended only by women and small children. The most important symbols of newly adult status conferred by *shahla ge* are the splitting of the girl's single braid into two braids tied up in a headdress, changing her bead or shell earrings for silver, and changing her two-tiered girls' skirt into the three-tiered, full-pleated skirt of the adult woman.

The Nuosu adult woman's "hundred-pleated" skirt is long enough to brush the ground and has three tiers: the top one is the waist, the second is cylindrical, and the bottom one is very full, composed of many small vertical pleats, sometimes numbering well over a hundred. Young women like to be flamboyant and use red, pink, yellow, green, and other bright colors together, with strong contrasts. Middle-aged and older women use more muted colors for a more dignified look. The most flamboyant is the Suondi style, with a multicolored band on top of the bottom section of the skirt (pl. 14). Some women in Leibo also wear skirts with unique patterns (pl. 15). Women's skirts in other areas usually have a series of single-colored bands (pls. 6, 10), traditionally made of woven wool, with the middle cylindrical section rather longer and usually red, and the bottom section black or dark blue but with narrow bands of red, white, black, or green interspersed, and sometimes little green pleats on the hem. When a woman walks, the pleats swish and swirl lightly, expressing feminine elegance. In Yanyuan County, older women's wool skirts are made in simple but elegant colors, in heavy cloth, and create an impression of stability and substance (pl. 16) .

Pant Legs: Big, Medium, and Small

Nuosu men's lower clothing is always long pants sewn out of light blue cloth. Their style, however, differs regionally.

The trouser legs of the Yynuo men are particularly wide—stretched out, many are a meter wide, the widest nearly two meters, using up to sixteen meters of cloth (pl. 5). Because at first glance these trousers look like a skirt, Yynuo are sometimes known as the "people of the big pant legs." Shynra trouser legs are smaller, usually two-thirds to one meter wide, so they are called "medium pant legs" (fig. 3.2). Suondi trouser legs are very narrow, just large enough to put a foot through, so they are called "horse pants" or "small pant legs" (fig. 3.3).

The large and medium pant styles feature a twelve-centimeter dark-colored band on the hem, often with decorative borders, and three round decorations on the crotch. The small trousers are relatively free of decoration, but the seams are clearly visible. Each of these trouser styles, when coupled with the decorated jacket that closes on the right side, expresses the free and martial ideal of Nuosu manhood.

Colorful Decoration of Clothing

Both men's and women's jackets have front panels that button on the right. Nuosu people can immediately tell someone's hometown by looking at his or her jacket. Yynuo men's jackets are close fitting, with a short front and narrow sleeves. The sleeves, yoke, and edges of the jacket front are bordered with embroidered patterns, of which the crab claw is the most common, done in colors every bit as bright as those of women's clothing (pl. 28). Shynra men's jackets have a looser fit to the trunk, with a longer front and narrow sleeves (fig. 3.12). Around the shoulders and on the top edge of the front are insets in the cockscomb pattern, using harmonious and tasteful colors. Suondi young men's jackets are short, reaching only to the navel. They often have silver buttons with brightly colored loops, to catch the light and add color to otherwise plain garments (fig. 3.18).

Most women's garments also have a front panel that buttons on the right, and are decorated on the front panel, sleeves, hems, yokes, collars, and buttonholes with cross-stitching, embroidery, inserts, and decorative borders in a great variety of colors and patterns. Women wear long-sleeved jackets, overcoats, long gowns, vests, and sleeveless jackets. Vests from Yuexi and Xide Counties in the Shynra district are decorated with strips of rabbit fur around the armholes and the collar (pl. 10). Women's vests from Ganluo feature frog-buttons straight down the front and are decorated all around the shoulders with very intricate patterns, using cross-stitching, appliqué, inserts, and flat embroidery (pl. 17). The patterns are mostly flowers, many of which repeat symmetrically.

3.18. Buttons on a Suondi man's jacket

Plate 1. The styles of clothing displayed in *Mountain Patterns*

Plate 3. Multicolored eave decorations
extending the length of a house

Plate 2. Carved patterns on interior walls. (Photo by Stevan Harrell)

Plate 4. Detail of a brightly
painted eave decoration

Plate 5. Yynuo "big pant legs,"
which require several meters of cloth

Plate 6. Unmarried Yynuo woman hand-spinning wool.
(Photo by Stevan Harrell)

Plate 7. Sleeves of a Yynuo jacket, showing several couched patterns

Plate 9. Shynra headcloth with cross-stitched patterns

Plate 8. Unmarried Suondi woman

Plate 10. Young married Shynra women's dress. (Photo by Stevan Harrell)

Plate 11. (*below*) Suondi-style short felt jackets, dyed and undyed

Plate 12. Child's hat

Plate 13. Child's hat

Plate 14. Unmarried Suondi woman from Yanbian. (Photo by Stevan Harrell)

Plate 15. Colorful skirt patterns from Leibo

Plate 16. Middle-aged woman's skirt from Yanyuan, made of wool with natural dyes. (Photo by Stevan Harrell)

Plate 17. Female dancers wearing Ganluo-style vests

Plate 18. Shynra women gathered at a wedding, wearing both unmarried women's *uofa* and married women's *uoly*. (Photo by Stevan Harrell)

Plate 19. Yynuo unmarried women's *uofa*

Plate 20. Military tunic. (Photo by Bamo Qubumo)

Plate 21. (*below, left*) A *cheti*, or rice dish, hand-turned and painted in Apu Village. (Photo by John Putnam)

Plate 22. (*below, right*) A *kuzzur*, or soup tureen, from Apu. (Photo by John Putnam)

Plate 23. Painting designs on lacquerware. (Photo by Stevan Harrell)

Plate 24. Lacquered ram's horns, painted by Jjivo Vuqie. (Photo by Stevan Harrell)

Plate 25. Lacquered buffalohide bowl. (Photo by John Putnam)

Plate 26. Factory-turned lacquerware, still hand-painted

Plate 27. Artist and entrepreneur Jjivo Vuqie (right) and Stevan Harrell with some wares from Vuqie's factory. (Photo by Bamo Ayi)

Plate 28. Young Yynuo man wearing a *mohne ashy*, or amber earring with tassel, and a hero's belt with shell ornaments. (Photo by Bamo Qubumo)

3.19. Young Suondi woman's *uofa*

Distinctive Styles of Women's Headdresses

Nuosu women pay great attention to headdresses. They
differ not only from place to place, but also according to
the reproductive status of the woman. In general, adult
women who have not yet borne children wear *uofa*, or
headcloths; mothers wear *uoly*, or hats. There are many
different styles. *Uofa* tend to be brighter and more elaborate
than *uoly*, and demonstrate the needlecraft skill of the
wearer at its most elaborate and meticulous. Young Yynuo
women's *uofa* often consist of piles of cloth topped by decorative embroidery or elaborate hats, Shynra versions are
known for their "ladder" shape, and Suondi women are
famous for their cross-stitching. Many different styles
exemplifying young women's creativity with the needle are
presented here (pls. 18, 19; fig. 3.19; see also pls. 6, 8, 9, 10,
13, 14, 17).

Middle-aged and older women's hats are usually black,
with minimal decorative color, and come in a great variety
of shapes and sizes. Particularly noteworthy are the lotus-
leaf hats of the Yynuo (fig. 3.20) and the bamboo coil hats
of the Suondi.

3.20. Married Yynuo woman's lotus-leaf hat

Some large Nuosu households are managed not by men
but by a designated female, often a particularly ethical and
capable unmarried woman, whose position has a gravity
lacking in those of other women. The female manager

wears on her head a square headcloth with a strip of dark cloth that reaches below her shoulders and sways in the wind.

Belts and Lotus Purses

Nuosu also pay attention to what they wear around the waist. Belts are made of cotton, woven wool, or silk. There are decorative tassels on both ends of the belt, and patterns are often worked on its surface. Older people use black, blue, or other dark-colored cloth, while young people favor red, white, or gray. Belts are usually between one and 1.5 meters long by about five centimeters wide and are knitted at the waist, with the loose end allowed to hang down. Some men like to carry knives or silver snuffboxes in their belts.

Women often hang a triangular "lotus purse" made of brightly colored cotton from their belt. The layered purse is often red on the inside and black on the outside, decorated with various brightly colored patterns (fig. 3.21). From the bottom are suspended five different-colored streamers. This purse is not only useful for carrying things but is a popular fashion accessory. Some women also hang a tiny embroidered bag on their lotus purse.

Nuosu young men's shoulder bags are square, sewn of black and white cloth, decorated on both sides with colored stitchery or with four-way symmetrical designs sewn on with thin strips of colored cloth. The bottom is fringed or decorated with several hanging cloth strips (fig. 3.22).

Middle-aged and older men often carry a little crescent-shaped bag made of deerskin, with a cover that opens at the top and a leather button on either end. It hangs below the waist in front and contains tobacco leaves, a little tobacco pouch, tinder, and flint and steel for lighting a fire (fig. 3.23).

Bare Feet, Leggings, and Straw Sandals

Nuosu walk everywhere, and in the old days everyone—old and young, male and female—went barefoot most of the time. The soles of their feet were tough

3.21. (*above*) Triangular lotus purse, hung from the belt

3.22. (*left*) Shoulder bag

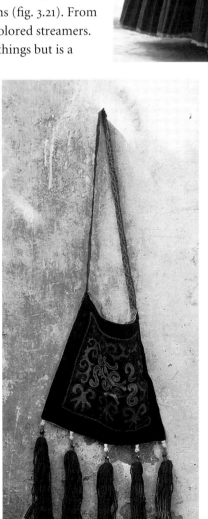

and strong, and they did not fear splinters but walked proudly, over mountains and through passes just as if they were walking on flat ground. Traditional footwear, including *jyxy*, felt socks, and leggings, was worn mostly in the wintertime to protect against cold. Recently, wearing shoes (usually bought from Han traders) with or without socks has become common.

Jyxy are sandals whose soles are made of wild plants, corn husks, hempen cord, or bamboo peel and whose straps are plaited of hemp. Felt socks are made from sheep's wool specially rolled for this purpose. Shaped like boots, and sometimes reaching as high as the kneecap, they come in both soled and soleless versions. Usually they are worn together with *jyxy* (fig. 3.24).

3.23. Deerskin tobacco pouch

3.24. Straw sandals with felt socks

Leggings are made of cotton cloth or woven from wool, usually about two meters long by ten centimeters wide, and are black, white, or gray. They were usually worn by men, wrapped around the calf from bottom to top.

The Caste System and Respect for Black

That Nuosu have long valued the color black is evident in ancient Chinese sources. Today the most obvious manifestation of this is the preference for black in clothing—cloth and felt are usually dyed black or dark blue, both of which are called *nuo* in Nuosu. This preference is an outward manifestation of the strict caste order of Nuosu society. For example, in the Suondi area, members of the aristocratic *nuoho* caste preferred to dress all in black, indicating their

high social position and the strictness of the caste order. *Nuoho* women often wore a black head covering and jacket, without decoration, with no color on the jacket, and only a stitched black border, which from a distance looked solid black. The hems of skirts were bordered in black, and older women wore all-black skirts (fig. 3.25).

Remnants of the caste system can still be seen in the colors, patterns, and style of clothing. For example, Yynuo aristocratic young women wear headcloths with more layers than those of commoners. Their collar-plates are made of heavy, dark-red woolen cloth, with the collar itself featuring an embroidered vortex pattern of brightly colored (primarily yellow) silk. Commoner women may not exceed their station by using this pattern. An aristocratic bride's head covering must be made of dark-colored, thin woolen cloth, with a white eagle feather stuck in the top to express her nobility, whereas a commoner woman's head covering is made of brightly colored silk. Aristocratic women who have borne children wear a larger hat than those worn by commoners. Aristocratic women's jackets and skirts are long, with as many pleats as possible (the higher the woman's

3.25. High-caste woman (right), dressed almost entirely in black

status, the more pleats), and the black strip sewn onto the hem of the skirt is broad. Women of the aristocracy and ruling families wear skirts long enough that their feet do not show, and when they walk haughtily, there is the sound of their skirts sweeping along the ground. Commoner women's skirts do not extend below the ankle, partly to make working more convenient.

Aristocratic Yynuo men's turbans are wrapped neatly, with a little tassel over the right ear, attached to the turban at the top (pl. 28). In general, aristocrats' clothing is more somber and correct, while commoners' is less strictly prescribed. For example, in the Suondi area, where the men's trouser legs are very narrow, commoners may put a little slit in the bottom and use a button to fasten the pant leg, whereas aristocrats may not. Nor may the latter wear hempen pants, but only wool or cotton.

Martial Tradition and Glory

The Nuosu have a long military tradition, stemming perhaps from the Yi peoples' migration several thousand years ago from the north to their present homeland, during which they encountered many enemies. The Yi-language historical text *Account of the Southwestern Yi* captures the Yi martial spirit well: "Like fierce tigers chasing horses, like wolves catching pigs, like eagles catching chickens, we pursue and slaughter our enemies." The same text also mentions military equipment that was used until the 1950s in Liangshan: tunics, spears, shields, and bugles. Other traditional military equipment used until recently in clan feuds included capes, suits of armor, arm-guards, war pants, and leg-guards. The materials used in making military clothing were very important, and the workmanship both fine and sturdy. A tunic, for example, required four colors of Tibetan-style wool cloth—red, blue, black, and white—and was rimmed with woolen serge and stuffed with a layer of cotton wadding. The tunic was closely fitted together —heavy, thick, and tough—and could fend off arrows. It had a round collar, short sleeves, and a fastener on the right (pl. 20).

Military overcapes made of silk were worn by commanders in order to distinguish their special position in the field. Arm-guards—made of felt or hide, decoratively rimmed with strips of black, white, and red cloth—were worn on the forearm, with the curved part fitting over the elbow. They protected against wounds from knives or spears. Fighting pants, also made of felt, were long enough to cover the knees, and on the front of the thighs were decorated with sewn strips forming the words "martial spirit"

in the Nuosu script. Some suits of armor, helmets, wrist-guards, and elbow-guards were made of water-buffalo hide and painted in the traditional lacquer colors of black, red, and yellow (fig. 4.6).

To this day, in Nuosu funeral rituals young men wear the tough, heavy armor and military clothing, along with leggings, and carry knives, swords, and shields, presenting an array of military might and bravery. They do military dances of attack and defense, accompanied by martial songs, such as the one that says,

Go, go quickly, go quickly, you ghosts.
I have horns on my head that will gore you,
And a knife in my hand that will cut you in half.

This dance helps the soul of the deceased pass the many dangers it encounters on its way back to the land of the ancestors.

3.26. An old couple in their "longevity" (funeral) clothes. (Photo by Stevan Harrell)

Cremation Clothing

When Nuosu die, they are cremated on a pyre of fir and pine wood, nine layers for a man and seven for a woman, with a man lying on his left side and a woman on her right. Rituals are performed to send the soul back to the land of the ancestors, from which the Yi peoples originally came. When people pass middle age, they begin to prepare their own funeral clothes. When someone dies, relatives wash the body and comb the hair, and dress the body in a complete suit of funeral clothes from head to toe, in order to maintain the respectable appearance of the deceased until the body is cremated. Usually, a man is dressed in a jacket and trousers, with a felt cape, white leggings, and a silk turban. The turban is tied into a "hero's horn" wrapped clockwise, the opposite direction of that used by living men. A woman should have a new jacket and skirt, a new felt cape, and a new lotus-leaf hat. Of the whole suit of funeral clothes, the most important item is the set of two jackets—a white one worn inside a black one. The funeral clothing should be primarily white, blue, and black. Red, yellow, and other bright colors are forbidden, lest the soul might encounter ghosts on the way back to the land of the ancestors (fig. 3.26).

After a person has died, the carefully prepared funeral clothes will be transformed along with the body into black smoke and will accompany the deceased back to the land of the ancestors, just as described in a text recited by *bimo*:

The harrier in the sky can see the horse's footprints.
Herd horses along with your ancestors;
Rest where they rest;
Look for their footprints and go forward.

[Translated by Stevan Harrell]

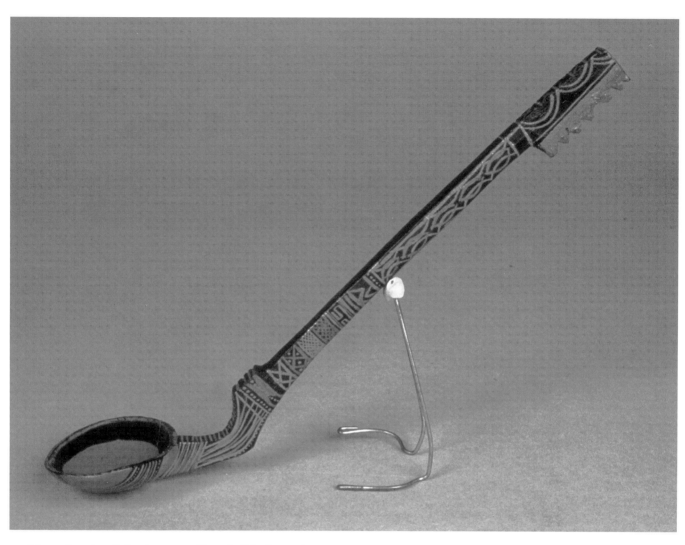

4.1. *Ichyr*, or long-handled eating spoon. (Photo by John Putnam)

Lacquerware

STEVAN HARRELL

NUOSU LACQUERWARE IS UNIQUE IN ALL THE WORLD. The color scheme of red and yellow on a black background; the designs of circles, rectangles, lines, and dots, as well as the swirling "cow's eye" pattern; and the shapes of the wooden objects—especially the wine cups with eagle's claws as feet, dove-shaped and round drinking vessels with sipping tubes, the pedestaled dishes, and long-handled, flat-bowl soup spoons—are like nothing else in southwest China or southeast Asia. The lacquered objects featured here represent a wide variety of materials, styles, and functions, indicating origins in different parts of Nuosu country. *Mountain Patterns* includes both traditional items, produced for hundreds of years and still made today, and modern items, factory produced by machine in a variety of shapes and functions far removed from older Nuosu uses and customs, but still drawing on customary patterns and using the familiar black, red, and yellow color scheme.

Traditional Lacquerware Manufacture

Apu Village in Xide County is a traditional site where members of the Jjivo clan have been making wooden lacquerware for at least nine generations.

Lacquerware artisans begin by selecting wood. Wood suitable for larger pieces—such as rice dishes (*cheti*; pl. 21), meat platters (*shepi*), and soup tureens (*kuzzur*; pl. 22)—comes from the *ngehni* tree, a species of birch that grows only in untouched forests and only partway across the county, so that villagers have to buy chunks of that wood from people who live nearer the forests. For smaller pieces, such as bowls and long-handled spoons (*ichyr*; fig. 4.1), artisans use rhododendron wood, which they gather locally. Whatever kind of wood they use, they must first cure it by burying it in the ground so that the wind cannot reach it and it dries slowly.

The Jjivo make their dishes on a pit lathe, or *gedde*. When a man wants to make a dish, he selects and cleans a blank from his underground storage pit and carves out a small hole in the center of one side, using an adze, or *zzo*. He then takes a mallet, made from a section of a pine trunk cut so that a thick branch makes a convenient handle, and pounds the metal point on one end of the *zzowo*, or rotor shaft, into the hole in the blank. The *zzowo*, with the wooden blank attached, fits into two bearings, each attached to a sturdy wooden rail on one side of the lathe pit. The flat end of the *zzowo* fits into a ball bearing (a recent innovation) on the left-hand rail; the wood blank attached to the other end is pounded onto a plain steel bearing point, or *funzoddu*, on the right-hand rail (fig. 4.2).

4.2. Setting the rotor into the lathe bed. (Photo by Stevan Harrell)

4.3. The turner working with his chisel while two men pedal the lathe. (Photo by Stevan Harrell)

To set the rotor in motion, a belt (formerly leather, but now made from a more durable old tire) is looped around the *zzowo* and around a pair of two-meter-long wooden foot pedals. Two men sit on board seats placed above the middle and rear ends of the pit and push the pedals alternately to make the rotor spin (fig. 4.3).

The owner of the wood uses a set of tools called *iku* to turn the blank into the desired shape. These tools, like the *zzo* and *zzowo*, are made by an itinerant blacksmith to the order of the wood turners. A set of *iku* has about eight pieces—wooden shafts about one meter long, each with a chisel point of a slightly different shape on the end, so that turners can shape the insides and outsides of different kinds of dishes to different angles (figs. 4.4). When the dish has almost attained its desired shape, the pedestal where the wood attaches to the *funzoddu* usually breaks off, and the bottom of the dish, inside and out, has to be finished off with an adze (fig. 4.5). After the bowl is smoothed with abrasive, its newly exposed surfaces are allowed to dry for a few days, and then it is ready to paint.

In former times, the Jjivo made their own lacquer out of local plant pigments. They still do this for the black lac-

4.4. A bowl taking shape. (Photo by Stevan Harrell)

4.5. Finishing off a bowl with a *zzo*, or adze. (Photo by Stevan Harrell)

quer, which covers the entire dish as an undercoat. After the black dries, they apply commercial lacquer in intricate designs of red and yellow (pl. 23). Although only male clan members learn the craft of turning on the lathe, their wives sometimes learn to paint. The designs are traditional and have particular names, such as the cow's eye swirl and fish-net cross-hatching customarily painted on tureens (pl. 22) and meat dishes, and the cockscomb, chicken intestine, eggplant, firelighter, gold chain, and fingernail patterns found on rice dishes (pl. 21). Each painter assembles his or her own box of tools, including mixing dishes, paint

paddles, and an assortment of brushes, including the ones used to paint the finest lines and dots, made of three pig hairs attached to the end of a thin wooden stick.

In today's economy, the Jjivo lacquermakers can nearly double the income they would earn by farming alone. They sell some of their wares in the market at Mishi, about two hours' walk away, and at times people come to Apu to purchase the wares directly.

Apu is not the only place in Liangshan that traditionally produced wooden lacquerware; it was also made, in some-what different patterns, in Meigu, Zhaojue, and Ganluo. And turned wood is not the only material that can be painted with the colorful lacquer designs. Ram's horns, used as drinking vessels (pl. 24), are painted by the Apu artist Jjivo Vuqie, and others paint items made from water-buffalo hide. Most spectacular of these were the armor breastplates worn by warriors before the advent of firearms (fig. 4.6), the toughest, most arrow-resistant hide for which came from the water buffalo's legs. Saddles of wood, or wood and leather (fig. 4.7), are still in use, and perhaps most surprisingly, bowls are also made of buffalohide. The village of Hoggumo in Meigu County, in fact, still specializes in the manufacture of lacquered buffalohide bowls (pl. 25). Selected hides are soaked in water for several days until they are soft and then are molded into the desired shape. They are then dried, trimmed, and painted with lacquer. Finally, musical instruments such as panpipes (fig. 6.4) are deco-rated in similar patterns.

Lacquer in the Factory

Lacquerware has become more than a craft item or curios-ity in the land of the Nuosu. An object of everyday use, it is now mass produced in two different factories.

The oldest factory is in Zhaojue County, the former prefectural capital of Liangshan. It was started by a Han Chinese family, the Lans, who came to Zhaojue in the 1960s and built cheap, functional furniture. The Lans became interested in local crafts and began to explore the local villages, including those in the Bilur district where lacquer-ware was traditionally made. In the Cultural Revolution years they made a few functional dishes, but after the end of the cultural dark ages, when Nuosu arts and crafts were no longer discouraged but positively promoted by local governments, the Lan family factory began to adapt Nuosu designs to factory production. Since then, the factory has grown to a workforce of forty-four people, all but two of them Han, with yearly sales of about ¥600,000 and a profit of ¥40,000 in 1997.

4.6. Armor breastplates, lacquer on leather

4.7. Horse with a lacquered saddle

The other active factory is an outgrowth of the Jjivo clan's craft production of lacquerware in Xide County. It was started in 1981, and at its inception employed Jjivo Vuqie, one of the most accomplished Jjivo painters, as its artistic director. In 1994 it employed thirty-four production workers, mostly painters, all but two of them Nuosu. The scale of production was quite similar to that of the factory in Zhaojue.

We have included factory-produced wares from Zhaojue and Xide in *Mountain Patterns* precisely because they are not strictly traditional arts and crafts. They stand, instead, as an example of the ways in which old artistic patterns from Nuosu culture have been adapted to the modern commodity economy and to the tastes of modern consumers. The first thing to notice in viewing these objects (pl. 26) is that while the designs are closely derived from those on the village wares, the colors and finishes do not look quite the same as those produced in Apu and other villages. The yellow is brighter, and the texture, a combination of finer finishing and shinier paint, has a distinct gloss that is missing from the village wares. This yellow, in fact, was the cause of a dispute in the Xide factory. The original artistic director, Jjivo Vuqie, thought it increasingly inauthentic, so in 1991 he resigned from his post, raised some capital from his clan, and started his own factory as a private enterprise. His wares preserved the shine and the stylistic innovations of the original state-operated factory, but he replaced the bright lemon yellow with a duller, more traditional color (pl. 27).

But the main innovation in the factories is in the types of utensils they produce. Wooden lacquerware is no longer confined to a few types, but is now adapted to modern middle-class life.

Contemporary objects include dinner plates; chopsticks; teacups with covers, such as those used in northwest China and Japan; large long-stemmed beer goblets; several styles of candy dishes, some with tripod or single-stemmed bases; fifteen-centimeter-wide lidded containers for *go* game stones; covered, Japanese-style rice bowls; little round shallow containers that could hold paper clips or perhaps red seal-paste; revolving serving trays; rectangular serving trays; round and oval table tops; round and rectangular stools; lacquered ceramic vases and liquor bottles; and Nuosu-style drinking vessels, previously made either round or in the shape of a dove, but now fashioned as a stereotypically Chinese figurine of a water buffalo with a little boy riding on top. It may be significant here that in Nuosu symbology, oxen represent Nuosu; yaks, Tibetans; and water buffalo, Han.

Lacquer as Commodity

One reason why the factories in Zhaojue and Xide have been so successful and are expanding their sales yearly is that lacquerware, uniquely among the Nuosu cultural products featured in *Mountain Patterns*, has successfully entered the modern commodity market. Not saddles or armor, of course: saddles are of use only in the hills, and armor is a rare ritual good and collector's item. But dishes, in both their traditional and their new forms, have taken off as middle-class housewares. They have done so in somewhat different ways for Nuosu and for outsiders.

There are now considerable numbers of middle-class Nuosu urbanites, particularly in Xichang and in the county seats around Liangshan Prefecture. Most of them are teachers, cadres, and other government employees. Their houses and apartments, like those of their Han neighbors and co-workers, almost always contain low glass-fronted shelves for display of artifacts and curios. In a Nuosu household of this sort, the artifacts will almost always include lacquer cups, used for serving liquor to guests (liquor will often be served in a Nuosu household in more or less the same way as Han people serve tea), and often larger dishes that are primarily for display. When Nuosu families choose to extend traditional hospitality on a special occasion, such as a wedding or engagement, they will often replace the Chinese food they eat daily with an ethnic specialty and kill a pig (or, if they can find one, a sheep) to boil and serve to guests in the usual Nuosu fashion—cut in chunks and served in a *shepi*, even though their table service may include such nontraditional utensils as chopsticks, themselves decorated with black, red, and yellow lacquer (fig. 4.8). In this way, even though they live a typical Chinese middle-class life, Nuosu urbanites have a symbolic connection to their artistic heritage, an ethnic marker that, unlike traditional clothing (which seems out of place in an urban setting), fits right into the turn-of-the-millennium Chinese penchant for gracious urban living.

But not all of the customers for Nuosu lacquerware at the urban department stores and smaller private shops are themselves Nuosu. Lacquerware that has entered the commodity market is available to anyone who wants to buy it, and it is still very inexpensive. For Han or other urbanites, it is attractive not so much because of its ethnic connotations but because of its novelty and its plain aesthetic appeal. In addition, ethnic goods have become popular as official gifts given by Chinese government institutions to foreign visitors or overseas hosts, and the Zhaojue factory now does considerable business selling to these bureaus and departments. And, of course, foreign tourists are always looking for ethnic arts and crafts to take home as exotic souvenirs. For these customers, as for urban Nuosu, lacquerware is relatively inexpensive, attractive, and potentially useful.

4.8. Banquet at an urban Nuosu household. (Photo by Stevan Harrell)

We thus have the interesting phenomenon of an "ethnic art" that in some cases is produced and consumed by people who are not members of the ethnic group. One might decry this as inauthentic, or one might laud it as an example of a contribution made by the Nuosu to Chinese—or even to world—culture.

Silversmithing and Jewelry

BAMO QUBUMO

Nuosu society has long respected the position of skilled artisans, or *lygur*, who include lacquermakers, silver- and goldsmiths, felters, saddlemakers, stone carvers, carpenters, and straw-raincoat makers. Among the most respected are silversmiths—usually men—who apprentice themselves to masters, while others carry on generations-long clan traditions, as in Lurbu and Yomuho Villages in Meigu County, where many pieces featured in *Mountain Patterns* were made.

Silversmiths use over one hundred different tools, including the sheepskin bellows; the charcoal-fired forge; the melting crucible; the quenching bowl; various casting-molds, pitch boards, chisels, hammers, awls, and shears; and many different sizes and shapes of punches (fig. 5.1). The various processes employed by silversmiths can be seen in the sequence of steps followed in manufacturing a decorated collar with semispherical silver studs.

The smith first melts some silver and casts it in the shape of a strip twelve to fifteen centimeters long, which is pounded to the thickness of two sheets of paper. He then puts it on the lap-held pitch board and with a hollow, broad-pointed chisel breaks off little pieces, the rounder and more even the better. He puts the little silver disks in a round, cast-iron dapping die and uses a wooden dapping punch, thick as a chopstick and ten centimeters long, to pound them into a concave shape, and then returns them to the mat and makes a little hole in each one with an iron punch, so that they can be sewn onto the collar. To make the silver studs even prettier, he can return them to the copper crucible and heat it, rinse the studs in alum water, and rub them with a cloth to make them shiny and bright.

In addition to clothing decorations, Nuosu silversmiths also make eating and drinking utensils, many types of jewelry, snuff boxes, inlaid silver saddles, silver-decorated officers' capes and caps, and silver-decorated bridal veils and dresses.

5.1. Master silversmith Shama Qubie at his forge. (Photo by Stevan Harrell)

Silver Vessels

Nuosu silver utensils are used together with lacquer ones and come in most of the same shapes, except that silver eating utensils, other than small bowls, have always been quite rare and used only by the aristocracy. Silver drinking vessels, on the other hand, have always been popular and are closely connected with ritual and mannerly entertainment. Alcoholic beverages occupy a prominent place not only in the culinary culture but also in the manners of social interaction. When guests come to the door, they are invited to sit in the most honored places and are offered liquor; dispute settlements and treaties are sealed with liquor; when discussions of major issues reach consensus, liquor confirms it; and liquor is even more intimately associated with marriages, funerals, festivals, prayers, and sacrifices. No wonder drinking vessels are so rich and plentiful in Nuosu culture.

In addition to silver drinking vessels made in the same shapes as lacquer vessels, some are shaped like birds, primarily doves, pigeons, and sparrows (fig. 5.2). The body is round or oval, and the wings are often spread out flat. The beaks come in different sizes, wide or narrow, some sticking straight out and some hanging down, portraying different postures. The birds' legs are often pipes into which

wine is poured; one drinks from the beak, from a little hole in the top of the head, or from a tube in the bird's side, half concealed below the wings. The heads on some vessels are decorated with colored wild-bird feathers or with strips of red cloth, so that they resemble phoenix heads. Some have sets of little tubular chimes hanging from the side of the beak, which jingle when the vessel is moved.

There are also fish-shaped drinking vessels, which are oval in shape, like a fish lying on its side. Liquor is poured in through a hole in the tubular base beneath the fish's belly, and one sips through the fish's mouth. A silver plate for a dorsal fin, either perpendicular or oblique to the body of the fish, makes the fish appear to be swimming in the water.

Silver Jewelry

Although Nuosu like both silver and gold jewelry, they prefer silver. It complements their brightly colored clothing, lending charm to young women, dignity to middle-aged and old women, and martial glory to men. Varieties of silver jewelry include head, hat, and clothing ornaments; earrings; finger rings; bracelets; collars; and necklaces with large pendants hanging down the front or sometimes even the back (figs. 5.3–4). Nuosu women associate beauty

5.2. Silver dove drinking vessels, made by master silversmith Loge Nyupu. (Photo by John Putnam)

5.3. Upper-caste woman with head ornaments

5.4. Silver necklace with ornaments on the back

with lots of silver jewelry, which makes people think of the moonlight: a beautiful Nuosu woman is "a daughter of the moon."

Bridal Trousseaux

According to tradition, a Nuosu bride should prepare her own wedding clothes, doing every stitch of the decorative needlework herself, but she is not allowed to sew the pieces together. She must wait until an auspicious day seven days or so before the wedding to invite a *bimo* priest and her friends from the village to sit together in her courtyard, starting at sunrise, and finish sewing the bridal clothes. The afternoon of the day the clothes are finished, the *bimo* performs a ceremony of blessing, after which the bride begins seven days of fasting. During the fast, village women come to her house every evening to sing "laments for the family" until she and her relatives are met by a delegation from the groom's household, and they take her away.

All of the items worn by the bride are made by her family, and many of them are passed from mother to daughter over several generations.

HATBANDS (UOGA)

Loose hair is gathered into a ponytail, bound with a red string at the back of the head, and wrapped with a head-cloth and twisted into a hat shape, onto which are tacked two hatbands. The topmost layer of the band is a long strip

of red woolen cloth, onto which is sewn seven square plates of gold or silver decorated with stamped or inlaid patterns, so that the red cloth and the shiny plates set each other off (fig. 5.5).

5.5. Bridal headband with silver plates

EMBROIDERED HEAD COVERINGS (HLIFU OR HLIMBO)

Usually when Nuosu women are married, they must wear a complete head covering, called *hlifu* or *hlimbo*. It is sewn together out of pieces of brightly colored cloth or embroidered cloth into a radial shape with a round or square peak, and is topped with an eagle or pheasant feather and hung with Job's tears. It represents celebration, avoidance of evil influences, and benediction (fig.5.6).

5.6. Fitting a bridal head covering (*hlimbo*). (Photo by Bamo Qubum

OVER-VEILS (*UOVIE*)

Brides from noble families added another layer, the *uovie*, on top of the head covering. One of the many styles features three levels of decoration: on top is a silver plate in the shape of a peacock spreading its wings, below which are eight small silver plates; in the middle layer silver plates with birds' head designs alternate with plates bearing ox-horn designs; in the bottom layer are plates that look like rams' heads seen straight on; and capping the whole veil is a little bird made of silver (fig. 5.7).

BRIDAL NECKLACES (*ZIZIFU*)

The *zizifu* is the most valued piece of bridal jewelry in the Suondi area. Up to a meter long and weighing as much as three kilograms, it includes eight separate pieces of sil-

verwork. It is made primarily of silver links and is worn around the neck. The bottom piece is a silver crescent with decorative stamped patterns of sun, moon, stars, reptiles, and birds; it is sometimes hung with bunches of silver tubes. The other pieces are various silver plates hung with tassels of silver tubes, each with different stamped patterns. The tubes serve as chimes that sound when the bride walks (fig. 5.8).

Decorative Patterns on Silver

Early Nuosu designs used for decorating silver were the same as those used on lacquerware, traced free-hand and quite simple. Patterns were abstract representations of sun, moon, ram's horns, flying birds, insects, reptiles, and leaves. Later patterns resembling plants and animals tended to represent whole animals; more common were more abstract, purely decorative patterns made of dots and lines that depicted patterns of contrasting light and shadow. The body of the silver drinking vessel in figure 5.9, for example, is decorated with fine, closely packed, stamped, and filigreed patterns, the intricacy of which is set off by an undecorated space circling the middle. Curved and straight lines are used together to achieve an effect of transformation within overall unity. The art of silver decoration, compared with that of lacquerware painting, has thus undergone considerable development.

Colorful Styles of Jewelry

HEAD ORNAMENTS: CONICAL HATS AND HAIR BEADS

In Nuosu society, the conical "coolie" hat is also a kind of head ornament, and at clan meetings (*cyvi momge*) in the old days, only the leaders—*suyy* (political leaders) and

5.8. Bridal
necklace
(*zizifu*)

5.7. Bridal over-veil, or *uovie*. (Photo by Bamo Qubumo)

5.9. Silver drinking vessel

ndeggu (mediators)—were allowed to wear them, as they were a sign of status. Conical hats are woven of fine bamboo. Sometimes the crown is plaited into a cylindrical shape, which is then hung with silk threads (pl. 6). Some people plait the colored silk threads into patterns and cover the hat with them, or make a framework out of split bamboo in one of a number of possible shapes and wrap it with silk threads. Young Nuosu men and women both like these styles. Felt conical hats are made by placing a layer of black wool felt over a bamboo hat; some of these in turn are covered with silver plates in a variety of patterns, such as representations of myths. Originally, only *bimo* could wear such hats, but more recently any people of means may wear them (fig. 5.10).

Many young Nuosu women like to wear hair beads. They string a large number of silver, coral, or jade beads together and wrap them around their braids or hang them from the braids at the temples (fig. 5.11). In some areas women use hairpins made of bone, copper, silver, or gold, and they

5.10. *Bimo*'s felt-covered conical hat, decorated with silver plates. (Photo by Stevan Harrell)

5.11. Beads incorporated into the hairstyle with the headcloth

sometimes stick a crescent-shaped wooden comb into one of their braids, both as a decoration and to use to comb their hair.

EARRINGS

Both women and men wear earrings. Women pierce both ears, sometimes with one hole and sometimes with two, while men pierce only the left ear. Every year at sheep-shearing time, children have their ears pierced.

The fanciest dress of young Nuosu men includes amber beads (*mohne ashy*, or "yellow ear beads"). Shynra men wear two beads—one yellow and one red, with one red and one black cloth disk between the beads, and a long black-thread tassel hanging below. Suondi men wear a big yellow bead with seven or eight little red ones below it and a tassel hanging down. Yynuo men wear three beads, with a big yellow one in the middle and two smaller red ones above and below (pl. 28). Middle-aged and older men wear only a single silver ring.

Young women's earrings come in many shapes and sizes. Besides plain silver rings, there are several types:

bugu: rings made of jade, shell, coral, or silver, sometimes with the larger rings passing through smaller ones
hnaze hnavu: silver or gold dangles in a variety of shapes and lengths (fig. 5.12)
mohne: like the amber beads worn by men, and including the black tassel, but with smaller, red beads, usually numbering only three

5.12. Dangle earrings by master silversmith Loge Nyupu (Photo by John Putnam)

Other materials used for earrings are strings of coral or silver beads, silver chains, and silver floral patterns. Earrings are an important part of the Nuosu ideal of beauty. They may be big and bright, hanging down to the shoulders, swaying and enhancing the charm of a young woman when she walks; or long and dangling, mixing with braids and adding to the beauty of a married women; or small and delicate, playing off the color of the headdress; or hanging all around the head and neck, harmonizing with the collar plate and the embroidered collar, adding to the aura of elegance. In the past, young noblewomen wore inverted-sepal earrings, from which dangled fine braided silk-wire chains, each bearing a round disk or leaf-shaped plate at the bottom, which flashed scintillatingly as they walked (fig. 5.13).

COLLARS AND COLLAR PLATES

Nuosu women think of long necks as beautiful and emphasize neck decorations. They pay considerable attention to the collars of their jackets and make some collars separately, so that they can be worn with more than one jacket. All collars, whether for men's or women's jackets, are of the standup style and are made with many layers of colored cloth sewn together and decorated with needlework. The style of men's collars is relatively simple, with straight or curved patterns made of patchwork or appliqué (fig. 3.11).

Young women use red or other brightly colored cloth to make their collar facings, whereas middle-aged and older women usually use dark colors. Collar decoration is provided by silver collar plates (fig. 5.14) or silver collar studs, or by striped needlework patterns, evenly spaced cross-

5.13. Noblewoman's dangle earring

5.14. Silver collar plate, worn with long earrings

stitching, richly varying couching, or fine appliqué. The collar is closed by a silver collar plate or a set of three to five plum-blossom-shaped silver buttons. Collars coordinate with earrings hanging around the shoulder, so that when a young woman walks lightly or turns her head and smiles, she displays a pleasing elegance.

Hero's Belts and Bone Needlecases

When a Nuosu man wants to display his martial air to the fullest, he wears a hero's belt—which is plaited of soft cattle tendons and leather strings, decorated with round plates of clam or snail shells on the front, and lined on the sides with red cloth—hung diagonally over one shoulder. In the old days the belt held a sheath for the *yimo* long knife or the *hmiechu* short knife. Nowadays the knives and their sheaths have no military function and so have gradually lost their place in everyday clothing. The knife belt has evolved into an item of purely decorative clothing (pl. 28; fig. 3.12).

Women's chest adornments are somewhat simpler, usually consisting of a finely embroidered purse, a mouth-harp case, and a needlecase. The needlecase, which holds needle and thread, is made of bamboo, wood, or wool felt (fig. 5.15). Hollowed-out wooden ones are very rare. Mouth-harp cases and needlecases are usually made from a thin bamboo tube, carved on the surface with fine, even patterns. They may have colored pigments rubbed into the patterns or consist of several tiny bamboo tubes bound with leather and wrapped with colored wool or cotton thread, or be wrapped with hair from a horse's mane that is decorated by painting. Perhaps the most unique needle-cases are made of white cattle bone filed into a hollow cylinder and pierced with colored cloth, with a little embroidered lotus purse on the top end and five colored arrow-shaped cloth strips hanging from the lower end. The middle one can be pulled out to reveal a choice of needles for sewing.

Bracelets and Rings

Both men and women wear rings and bracelets. Men's bracelets are usually of copper or inlaid leather. The copper ones often feature simple patterns of sun and moon, eyes, or cockscomb and are believed to prevent strangulation by ghosts, arthritis, and other sicknesses. Inlaid leather bracelets are made in an unusual manner. The base is black or blue leather that is adorned with square, triangular, or circular studs of clamshell or animal bone.

Women's bracelets usually are made of silver (fig. 5.16), sometimes studded with small stones that make a swishing sound against their clothes when they move. Bracelets also may be made of stone, jade, amber, and other materials. In the Yynuo area there is also a kind of white bracelet made of a rare material called *hlyma*, which is said to be the bone of an animal that lives on snowcapped mountains.

Rings worn by men and women are basically the same, with differences only in size. All are made of silver, some set with coral, amber, jade, other stones, or *hlyma*. Many women also like to wear a pair of "saddle rings," which are long, in the shape of a saddle, with intricate silver patterns on the face, and are worn on the middle and ring fingers (fig. 5.17).

[Translated by Stevan Harrell]

5.15. Needlecases

5.16. Pair of linked silver bracelets

5.17. Saddle ring, worn with silver bracelets

Musical Instruments

BAMO QUBUMO

NUOSU HAVE MANY KINDS OF MUSICAL INSTRUMENTS, each with its own style, content, and manner of playing. They include wind instruments (the most common), bowed and plucked string instruments, and percussion instruments. Typical instruments in Liangshan include the mouth-harp, moon-shaped lute, *mabur*, panpipes, and end-blown flute. All are made of bamboo and preserve very old forms. The smallest is the mouth-harp, about five centimeters long. Even simple leaves can be used to play charming little tunes. Traditional Nuosu instruments have not succumbed to the onslaught of modern pop and electronic music, but continue to show remarkable vitality.

Nuosu proverbs tell us, "When we think of father, we play the flute; / When we think of mother, we play the mouth-harp," "The lute is my melancholy voice," and "To hear the sound of the *mabur* is to feel comfort."

Folk music is a traditional means of expression and interaction, of expressing feelings of joy and sorrow, and of transmitting the sounds of the soul. Nuosu people love music, which to them is like "the swift horse to the expert rider, or the spindle to the young maiden." In any Nuosu village you will find the sound of music; every young woman has a mouth-harp hanging around her neck, and young men often let their lutes speak for them. A witty elder will gain glory by showing how he can lift a lute from his back and play tunes over his head; a toothless old granny will take a mouth-harp away from nearby girls and play a couple of tunes; and little ones just learning to talk will begin to learn to play by imitating their elders.

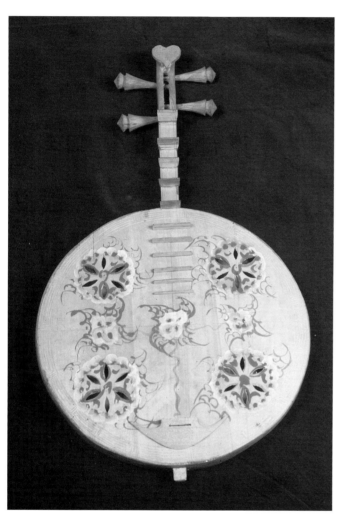

6.1. Four-stringed lute, or *pambie*

The Moon-Shaped Lute

The lute is called *pambie* in Nuosu, or just "strings," or the "frog lute." It is one of the most beloved instruments. In the valleys, by the campfires, and in the shingled houses, one hears the Nuosu lute. It is a sound like crying or storytelling, sometimes like a soft voice, evoking memories of images such as the calm surface of a lake in fall; sometimes strong and healthy, playing melodies that are like the crashing of waves; sometimes piling up poetic lines, rhymes that curl like a twisting stream in a dark forest. Those melodies that pluck the heartstrings, flowing from the fingers of an expert lutenist, are like the words of a Nuosu folksong:

Ten fingers plucking the lute—
It's not the lute talking
But the lutenist's heart.

Nuosu moon-shaped lutes are usually made out of carefully selected and decorated bamboo and wood. The front panel is usually made of walnut wood, with the bottom plate and neck made of yellow poplar (fig. 6.1). The neck is on the short side and the body large; the end of the neck is curved, often carved into a dragon's head or other design—even today dragon-headed lutes are considered the most valuable. Bamboo frets extend from the body up the neck. The strings are usually in pairs, either a single pair or two pairs tuned to the same two notes, and are made of horse-tail hairs or silk threads. The lute body may be round, hexagonal, or octagonal, with several small holes arranged in a pattern. Traditionally, the player does not use a pick, but plucks the strings with the forefinger and middle finger. The tone is relatively soft, but sweet and silvery. More recently, picks made of bamboo or ox horn have been used. These give a louder tone, and players can use varied picking and strumming techniques to expand the variety of their playing.

Traditionally in Liangshan, men play the lute and women the mouth-harp, but the famous female musician Shama Vurry, born in Leibo County in 1936, grew up hearing her brothers and uncles playing the lute and was the first to break custom and become a female lutenist.

The Bamboo Reed (*Mabur*)

The *mabur* is an instrument with a unique tone. It is made of a single bamboo pipe, about twenty to twenty-five centimeters long, with a mouth opening about five to six millimeters wide and seven finger holes. On the end, it has a flared trumpet made of ox- or ram's horn, which amplifies the sound. In the upper end is inserted a thin bamboo reed about nine centimeters long, which serves as a sounding piece. The peculiarity of playing the *mabur* is that while holding a long note, the player uses circular breathing, inhaling through the nose, allowing the diaphragm to continue to deliver air, with the result that there is no pause for breath between the notes. The tonal quality is thus mellow and soft, while the melodies are various and unique, and can imitate the crying of a child or the songs of birds. In addition to folk songs, the *mabur* is used to play sequences of rapid, fluid melodies. These are sometimes played without the amplifying trumpet so that the tone is very crisp, while the player uses rapid fingering to leap and ornament, so that the melody is bright and clear. There is also the two-reed style, in which the player creates music that is both louder and more stylized with a *mabur* with two reeds, which gives a unique sound.

The Mouth-Harp (*Hxohxo*)

The mouth-harp is the most widely spread plucked instrument in the Nuosu region. The proverb stating that "the mouth-harp can speak" perfectly expresses the uniqueness and infectiousness of mouth-harp music. Often several listeners will surround a player and guess what the instrument is "saying." When they have guessed correctly, the musician will play some more. This is not just musical play; it is also musical dialogue and spiritual conversation. Adults and children, men and women—all love the mouth-harp, and expertise with it is especially valued by Nuosu women. They often wear a mouth-harp container around their neck, so that wherever they go they can bring the sound that gladdens the heart. In the memory of every Nuosu woman, the sound curling upward from the mouth-harp, the gentle breeze ruffling the white buckwheat flowers, waving like a soft song and an easy dance in fields among endless mountains, is the magnificent image that accompanies her through life.

Mouth-harps are made of bamboo or copper. The bamboo ones are usually between ten and fifteen centimeters long and one centimeter wide, shaped like a short sword; the copper ones are between six and seven centimeters long and shaped like a leaf (fig. 6.2). Usually there are two or three leaves in the harp, but occasionally there is only one or as many as five. Usually there is an area cut out, in the shape of a chicken's tongue, in the middle of the leaf, called the "leaf tongue." The musician uses her thumb to pluck the end of the leaf, and the vibration of the leaf tongue produces a clear, sweet, melodious tone. The length, width,

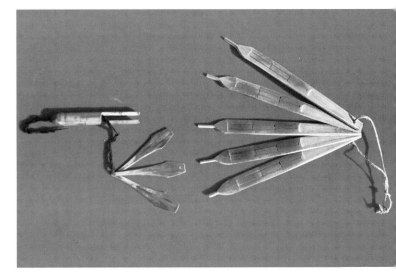

6.2. Two examples of the *hxohxo*, or mouth-harp

and thickness of the tongues are different, so the tone produced by each is somewhat different also. Craftsmen who make mouth-harps tune them carefully so that the sound of the leaves will harmonize properly. When playing the mouth-harp, the musician spreads the leaves out like a fan, and, holding the base of the leaves between her lips with her left hand, she uses her right thumb to pluck their tips. By using her mouth as a sounding chamber and by changing the configuration of her lips, tongue, and mouth, as well as by adjusting the size, tension, strength, and length of her breaths, she controls the tone, pitch, tempo, and loudness of each note, producing a rich, multilayered music. Each leaf, in addition to its fundamental note, can also produce a family of harmonics. The genius of the mouth-harp lies in its rich overtones and in changes of tone; the harmony of the overtone and the fundamental makes a multilayered but soft sound that one can listen to forever.

The End-Blown Flute (*Juhlur*)

The Nuosu-language text *Gguhxo*, which tells the story of the migration of the ancestors of the Nuosu into Liangshan, mentions both the end-blown flute and the mouth-harp: "They carried the flute in their belt and the mouth-harp in their hands."

The end-blown flute is a straight, thin bamboo tube featuring five to seven finger holes (fig. 6.3). The musician holds the top end against his front gums, biting the end of the flute firmly, and partially obstructs the opening with his tongue, spreading his mouth and blowing vertically. Rich variation in tone is produced by manipulating the shape of the mouth, tongue, and teeth and by controlling airflow. The flute can play every kind of folk melody; as soon as the player strikes up his tune, it reflects his mountain environment with its deep and leisurely melody. Because the musician's posture and the method of producing notes are unique, the end-blown flute is often called the "flute that you keep in your mouth." It is simple and unsophisticated, its origins are very early, and it has persisted to the present day.

The Panpipes (*Bbusse*)

There is a story about the origin of the panpipes: Long ago there was an old man who couldn't stop thinking about his five deceased sons. One day he was cutting green bamboo in the mountains and discovered that if he blew on a bamboo tube, it would make a sound. He then made five tubes of different lengths and stuck them into a gourd.

Playing them every day, it was like hearing the voices of his five sons.

The body of the instrument is usually made of a gourd, into which five to seven pipes are inserted (fig. 6.4). At the foot of each pipe is set a bamboo or copper reed; their lower ends protrude from the gourd, and in the middle of each is a finger hole. Usually each pipe can play two different notes—one with the hole covered, and the other (a major second or minor third lower) by covering the lower end of the tube with the thumb of the right hand. The panpipes play a pentatonic scale with a range of eight to ten notes. The Nuosu in Liangshan like to use short panpipes with a high range, but in areas where Nuosu live mixed with other ethnic groups, they have both high- and middle-range pipes.

The late elder musician Jjiejjo Vuqie was an expert player of many Nuosu folk instruments, including the mouth-harp, lute, *mabur*, and fiddle. As a boy he learned the skill of playing the pipes from a caravaneer. Later on, his skills and fame developed until he was famous and beloved all over Liangshan, and he became known as Jjiejjo Bbusse, or

6.3. Playing the *juhlur*, or end-blown flute

6.4. Panpipes (*bbusse*), lacquered in red, yellow, and black

"Jjiejjo the Piper." He taught the skills of playing and dancing to his son and to the official Liangshan Song and Dance Troupe.

The Two-Stringed Fiddle (*Fusse*)

The Nuosu name for the two-stringed fiddle is derived from *fu*, meaning "to rub, as with a bow." The sound box of the fiddle is usually made of oxhorn, covered with snakeskin or sheepskin, and the strings from horsetail hairs or silk thread. The bow is strung with horsetail hairs. There is no standard size. Most Nuosu fiddles are relatively small—less than thirty centimeters long, and shorter than the Chinese *erhu*.

Characteristics of playing style include much plucking and the use of harmonic ornamentation, using a multitude of short bow strokes with very few long notes. Young people are the main players and audience, because many old people say that the sound of the fiddle, *jysy jysy*, is like the word for "cutting of the ancestral line." But the instrument is still popular.

The Leaf

The playing of the leaf as an instrument is called *syrqi hmo*, "blowing the leaf." This is a primitive instrument, the simplest of all—leaves are everywhere, and both tree leaves and blades of grass will do for blowing. It is said that blowing the leaf originated as a means to call sheep; clever shepherds transformed these calls into exquisite melodies.

To play the leaf, one holds a leaf or a blade of grass with two hands, placing it against the front part of the upper gums (fig. 6.5). As one blows, the leaf vibrates and produces musical notes. One can also use two leaves stacked against the lips; when one blows, the stream of air forced out through the space between the two leaves vibrates them and produces a sound. The range of certain leaves can reach two octaves, and players can control the pitch, tempo, and dynamics of the sound with their breath. The most skilled players can even produce upper and lower harmonics, vibrato, and tremolo. Most melodies are repetitive. Leaves are easy to get, and men and women, old and young, all like to play for their own amusement. Because the tone is full and carries far, leaf-whistling can be used by shepherds to call scattered flocks of sheep or goats, or by lovers to send signals that they might be too shy to say face to face. One can also play simple folk tunes. Young men often use leaves to play sweet tunes of love and longing, so there is a folk song that goes,

Playing the leaf,
You must take advantage of its green youth.
Talking of love,
You must also take advantage of the green years of youth

Nuosu Music Today

In general, solo playing, which combines the functions of self-amusement and extemporaneous expression, is the only form of musical expression in the Nuosu core area.

6.5. Playing the leaf

Despite the antiquity of the instruments, most instrumental music has no established names for tunes or melodies. Only a few tunes have customary names. Some are named according to their mood, as in shepherding songs, laments, songs of tragedy, and songs of joy; and others according to their place of origin, such as Butuo, Ganluo, Jinyang, and Leibo tunes. Even though these tunes are played solo, they have developed a certain fixity of melody and structure. Because each instrument has its own tonal range and expressive abilities, each also has characteristic and commonly played tunes. Tunes from each district have a wide distribution. The Liangshan Song and Dance Troupe has developed traditionally based tunes for group performances. Nuosu performance groups—such as the rock groups Mountain Eagle and Black Tiger, and the rock singer Uojie Agi—are now familiar to the wider Chinese audience. Currently, modernized folk tunes are very popular in Liangshan, and the development of modern music is intimately connected with Nuosu folk traditions.

[Translated by Stevan Harrell]

The Bimo,
Their Books, and
Their Ritual Implements

MA ERZI

*B*IMO ARE HIGH-STATUS RELIGIOUS SPECIALISTS IN Nuosu society. Nuosu sometimes say, "If a ruler knows a thousand things, and a minister a hundred, then the things a *bimo* knows are innumerable." There is thus no better source of advice for living than the words of a *bimo*. *Bimo* recite all kinds of texts and perform all kinds of ceremonies: for the living they divine auspicious days and times, exorcise ghosts and expel evils, replace misfortune with good fortune, and regulate ethical behavior; and for the dead they provide offerings, lead the way to the world of the ancestors, and ensure peaceful rest in the next world.

The craft and knowledge of the *bimo* are certainly very ancient. According to the genealogy recorded in the book *Bipu*, which narrates the origin of the *bimo*, at the beginning of history there were thirty-seven generations of priestly practitioners, who constantly used and revised their craft until the profession entered its full maturity and perfected its skills at the time of Quobu Shyzu. From Quobu Shyzu the knowledge was passed on for twenty generations to one of the two recognized founders of Nuosu society in Liangshan, Agaqoni. From Agaqoni to the famous Adu Lypu to Asu Lazzi to the current octogenarian master Qubi Shomo (fig. 3.11), who drew the spirit pictures (figs. 8.6–8) for *Mountain Patterns*, is seventy-nine more generations. If we figure one generation at about twenty-five years, then the profession of *bimo* in its developed form has existed for about 2,500 years.

There are two kinds of *bimo*: those with orthodox succession and those without. Those with orthodox succession are called *bicy bimosse*, or hereditary *bimo*. According to the text *Bipu*, which has detailed genealogies, only certain clans—such as Jjihnie Ssehxie, Hma, Hxiesse Ssesuo, Pacha Sseshy, and Jjike Sseshy—have the requisite orthodox pedigree succession. *Bimo* without orthodox succession are those who acquired their knowledge only through apprenticing themselves to *bimo* of other clans and who are called *zzybi*, "those practicing an inappropriate craft" or "uncategorizable people." These *bimo* can do only ordinary rituals, not the large-scale rituals of *nimu cobi*, or rituals for the soul. Actually, though, this distinction is largely historically determined, so that the abilities of *zzybi* are not necessarily inferior to those of *bicy bimosse*, and some of the unorthodox *bimo* have superseded their orthodox colleagues, who thus have to look at things in a new light.

Bimo can also be classified according to the rituals they command as *gahxa bimo* and *gajjy bimo*, or high-road and low-road *bimo*, first- and second-rate. High-road *bimo* command the rituals of *nimu cobi*, including the *nra nimu* for people who died of old age or illness and who had children, the *ssy nimu* for those who died untimely deaths, the *cur nimu* for those who died of leprosy, and the *nyu ni re nimu* for people who died of consumptive tuberculosis and other lingering diseases. Low-road *bimo* primarily conduct rituals for casting spells, expelling ghosts, restraining ghosts, sending ghosts away, defending against ghosts, countering curses and spells, averting misfortune, divining auspicious days, and so on. There is no real sharp dividing line between the competencies of the two types of *bimo*, however, since many ritual situations require a combination of the two types, so that many individual *bimo* in fact serve in both capacities.

Bimo's ritual activity is inseparable from their texts and ritual implements, which are collectively called *ssymu ngagga*. The implements include *vytu*, *qike*, *kuhlevo*, *biju*, *bimo hxiekuo*, and various kinds of wild boar and deer teeth.

Ritual Texts

Texts are a *bimo*'s most valuable tools. The text *Bipu* says,

Bimo depend on their books.
The brown text pages,
Transmitted to sons and grandsons,
With their wise and perceptive words,
From the father to the son to hold dear.
The *vytu* and the *kuhlevo*
Are passed from elder to younger generation.

Perceptive people become mediators;
Brave men wield the knife and spear.
Rich people herd their cattle and sheep;
Our generations are intelligent and continue the *bimo* tradition
And chant the sound of texts.

Bimo evaluate each other's work on the basis of the number of texts they possess, and those who can understand texts written in many different hands are esteemed most highly. There are many different kinds of texts, whose contents touch on religion, philosophy, ethics, morals, astronomy, geography, history, and literature. At the most general level, texts can be divided into three large categories:

nisu: texts concerned with the rituals of *nimu cobi*, including pacifying the soul, purifying the soul, and sending the soul back to the ancestral home, all of which provide the deceased with a perfect rest and provide the living with a good future. Nuosu also call these rituals *zhymgusu*, assuring through ritual

that both the living and the dead can exist happily in their separate worlds.

ssyrrebburrre: texts containing spells or counterspells, whose primary purpose is to eradicate troubles caused by illness. These rituals are often classified as *namgusu*, "curing illness." Nuosu believe that ghosts cause illness, so they conduct these rituals to expel the ghosts and evil spirits that are haunting a person's body, and thus end misfortune. In other words, using ritual methods to control ghosts is equivalent to curing illness.

kusi hledu: texts for divination and fortune-telling

Bimo books were originally written on leather or white silk, but now almost all are written on paper, usually two spans long and over one span wide (fig. 1.4). They are bound with bamboo strips and can be rolled up when not in use, tied with strings, and wrapped in cloth or leather. Most books are written horizontally and from right to left, with no punctuation between sentences. A mark might be used to divide one section from another. Traditional ink is made by adding water to a mixture of pot soot and animal blood. There are two kinds of pens: a disposable kind, which uses an absorbent hemp stalk or stick of wood; and a quill produced by snipping off the end of a hollow bird-feather shaft and inserting fine hairs that are cut off squarely. Nuosu letters are written with no differences in the width of different kinds of strokes.

Ritual Implements

SPIRIT QUIVERS (*VYTU*)

The *vytu* is made of two lengths of hollowed-out cedar wood about five centimeters thick and thirteen centimeters long from top to bottom, put together in the form of a needlecase (fig. 7.1). The front section is called the male cedar, the back section the female cedar. The top end looks like a bear's snout with the mouth open. The size of the snout must match that of the mouth of the *bimo* who uses it, for if it is bigger than the owner's

7.1. *Vytu*, showing the male and female sections and the "bear's snout" shape of the top

7.2. *Bimo* Qubi Lysse demonstrating the manner of carrying the *vytu*. (Photo by Stevan Harrell)

7.3. A *qike* made of woven bamboo, with carved animals on the handle

mouth, it might overpower him, and if it is smaller, he will not be able to use his magical powers to their full extent. The *vytu* is lacquered all over on the outside and wrapped in gold, copper, or wool thread. The number of times it is wrapped depends on the caste of the *bimo*'s lineage: for a *nzymo*, it has nine wrappings, for a *nuoho* seven, and for a *qunuo* five. There is a small iron ring near each end, to which is attached a copper wire or other cord for the *bimo* to wear over his shoulder (fig. 7.2). Inside the tube are placed *lovy* or *malovy*, thin strips made of bamboo, of which there are two kinds. Those whose top end is carved into a Y shape are called female, and those cut diagonally at the top end are called male. When casting spells against ghosts, a *bimo* first reads the text about the origin of the *lovy* and then chants the name of the object of the spell while rubbing the *lovy* together in his hands, telling the ghosts to turn around and go in another direction, into the ghost town designated by the *bimo*.

SPIRIT FANS (QIKE)

There are two kinds of *qike*, made from bamboo and from copper. This is an oval-shaped fan, with a handle made from a single piece of cherry wood, in the shape of a crawl-ing snake, with carvings of tigers, frogs, otters, or other animals (fig. 7.3). On the one hand, images of eagles (representing the sky), tigers and wolves (representing the land), and otters or frogs (representing the water) show that the spiritual power of the *bimo* can overcome any obstacles of the sky, earth, and water. On the other hand, they show that the spirits of these animals can suppress evil and fight malevolence. Copper fans are beaten into shape and are used only for rituals exorcising leprosy ghosts. Bamboo fans are used in the *nimu cobi* rituals when calling the souls of the relatives or family members of the deceased or renewing the souls of the five grains. While chanting the ritual text, the *bimo* uses the *qike* to continually fan grains of rice or corn—the more the better—in the direction of the household members.

BIMO'S HATS (HLEVO OR KUHLEVO)

It is said that these were originally made of copper, but now they are usually made of an ordinary conical bamboo hat, covered with a layer of wool felt. Wealthy *bimo* sew gold and silver plates in a variety of designs on the felt. The *hlevo* is the emblem of *bimo* status. He has but to wear this hat and, wherever he goes, people—whether they are acquainted with him or not—will know that he is a *bimo*. They may approach him, if desired, to perform rituals for them (fig. 5.10).

SPIRIT BELLS (BIJU)

People often say about their belief that when the *bimo* rings the spirit bell in this world, in the world of the spirits there is a sound of clanging, indicating that spirits in the other-world are busy and stirring. The *bimo*'s ringing of the bell thus raises the spirits and also can suppress ghosts (fig. 7.4).

7.4. A *bimo*'s bell

STRING BAGS (HXIEKUO)

When *bimo* travel to do their rituals, they use the *bimo hxiekuo*, a bag plaited of hemp stalks, to carry their ritual implements and texts. It is forbidden to use the *bimo hxiekuo* to carry anything else. Conversely, the texts and ritual implements cannot be carried in any other kind of bag; in fact, the *hxiekuo* itself has a sacred meaning, so every *bimo* must have one.

OTHER OBJECTS

Bimo often wear a necklace made from two long boars' teeth. Tradition has it that the best teeth are from boars who live in deep, wild mountain valleys uninhabited by people, and who have died natural deaths; boars killed by hunters are only second best. *Bimo* also wear a necklace made of a pair of teeth from a male river deer, tied tightly together and sewn up with cloth, with a pretty cloth band; this can also be used as a decoration for ritual implements. Some implements are decorated with a stretched-out eagle's claw that is treated with preservative and sewn on with a cloth band. These decorations repel evil spirits and ghosts.

Classification of Rituals

Rituals are conducted in specially prepared ritual spaces, whose arrangements are complex and varied. A *bimo* must know for a particular ritual what texts to read, what melody and rhythm to use in reading them, which elements go first, what kind of animals need to be sacrificed, how the spirit sticks are to be arranged in the ground, what spirit pictures and ghost boards should be painted and how, and how ghost effigies should be constructed. There are complex and stringent rules for each of these, and they must be followed exactly if benefits are to come to both the *bimo* and the client. Otherwise, as the saying goes, "If the sacrifices and spirit sticks are insufficient, the client may be harmed; if the textual recitations are simplified, the *bimo* may be harmed." A complete explication is impossible here, but the chart below shows the general classification of rituals.

Nimu Cobi

A complete *nimu* ritual is extremely long and complex, and includes at least one hundred separate ritual acts and arenas. The shortest rituals might take a day and a night, while the longest take as many as nine or even twenty-one days and nights. Rich clients might sacrifice as many as one hundred animals—cattle, sheep, goats, pigs, and chickens—while the poor might only sacrifice a few. As the saying goes, "*Nimu* and weddings are not measured by absolute standards." Although the ritual may be made longer or shorter, one may not skip around at random. The most important parts are making the *madu* (spirit tablet), sending off the soul, and Joho.

MAKING THE *MADU*

After a mother or father has died, their sons and daughters choose an auspicious time and ask all of the people who perform cremations to go with them to a clean spot in the

---

CLASSIFICATION OF NUOSU RITUALS

Nimu Cobi (Rituals for the Soul)
  Madu (spirit vessel rituals)
    Nimu for people who died peaceful deaths
    Nimu for people who died violent deaths
    Nimu for people who died of leprosy
    Nimu for people who died of tuberculosis
    Nimu for dividing a clan
  Rituals of peace and harmony
    Prayers to spirits
    Adjustments to the soul
    Calling lost souls
    Cleansing

Rituals of Divination and Exorcism
  Exorcism
    Casting spells
    Exorcising ghosts
    Removing pollution
    Preventing epidemics
    Offerings
  Divination
    Osteomancy
    Ovomancy
    Hepatomancy
    Horoscopy
    Other divination

woods to find a tender shoot of bamboo. After making a few food offerings, they pull the shoot up and take it to a spot near where the parent was cremated and start a fire, wailing loudly, in order to wake the spirit of the deceased. They then take the bamboo to the remains of the pyre and turn it around several times, to represent rolling up the spirit on the bamboo, and they say, "On an auspicious day like today, we come to call your spirit to cross [to the other-world]." Then they bring the bamboo back to a *bimo* waiting nearby. The *bimo* cuts off a piece about one or two centimeters long and splits it lengthwise. He trims the top end of one part to make it into a *hxieqy*, a symbolic representation of the ancestor. The top end of the *hxieqy* is trimmed according to the sex of the ancestor—pointed for a man, flat for a woman (fig. 7.5). The other end is cut off flat for either sex, to stand on end without falling.

After this, knowledgeable people who help the *bimo* with the ritual wash fine wool, already prepared from an autumn shearing, clean it and purify it with alcohol, and then wrap the *hxieqy* in the wool; this is called "putting on clothes." In addition, they prepare a piece of hawthorn wood a little thicker than a man's thumb, cutting a hole in the top end and whittling the bottom end into a point. The *hxieqy*, already "clothed," is then inserted vertically into the hole and is wrapped in an inner layer of silk or hemp thread and

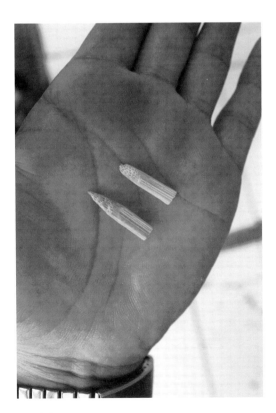

7.5. *Hxieqy*

an outer layer of hemp thread. This container, with the *hxieqy* inside, is the *madu*, or spirit vessel (fig. 7.7). Then the *bimo* places three sets of spirit sticks in the ground: black, colored, and white. The black group consists of thin branches with the bark on and symbolizes the dark path. The colored group consists of sticks with the bark half peeled and symbolizes the half-dark, half-bright path. The white group consists of completely peeled sticks and symbolizes the path of brightness (fig. 7.6). A model of a cremation pyre is built behind the white group. The *bimo* reads a text of offering while he takes the *madu* through the forest of black sticks, into the forest of colored sticks, and then through the forest of white sticks. He stops the *madu* on the cremation pyre, to symbolize the fact that the soul of the deceased, under the guidance of the *bimo*'s spirit, has left the mass of ghosts and moved step-by-step from their dark realm into the bright realm of spirits.

After this the *madu* is placed on top of a warrior's wrist-guard, which in turn is placed on top of a slab of burnt stone, where offerings of food and alcohol are made, and people chant,

Don't go to neighbors on the left and right to cause trouble;
Don't go to enemies' houses to cause trouble.
Here at home we have engaged a *bimo* to read scriptures and
    a *sunyi* to beat his drum.
Don't be angry;
There is no way you can become a ghost. . . .

Then the cremation handlers cut a hole in the roof of the house of the deceased and give the *madu* to the sons and daughters. More simple offerings are made inside the house, and then the *madu* is placed on a rectangular mat of bamboo slats, representing a bed for the soul (fig. 7.7). Before the soul crosses over, offerings are made inside the house. After the soul has crossed over, the *madu* is placed at a spot on a mountain cliff with *madu* of other ancestors of the clan.

SENDING OFF THE SOUL

Nuosu believe that a deceased soul can find peace—and avoid encounters with evil spirits that will eventually turn it into a ghost that bothers the world of the living—only if it returns to the land of the ancestors. According to tradition, the earliest homeland of the Nuosu of Liangshan was Zyzypuvu, near present-day Zhaotong, in northeastern Yunnan. So after someone dies, descendants lead the soul station by station, beginning with the current home and ending up with the original dwelling place of the ancestors.

7.6. Ritual arena for the *madu* rite in *nimu cobi*, showing black (rear), colored (middle), and white (front) paths

7.7. A complete *madu*, hanging inside a house in its bamboo mat

They advise the spirit as to where it should stop and rest, drink water, eat, water its horse, and stay overnight. They guide it as to the topography it will be passing through, the climatic conditions, what difficulties it might encounter at specific places, and what preparations it ought to make. There are many detailed texts for this kind of ritual, not only among Nuosu but among other Yi and related peoples, and it is possible that they also constitute records of the migration history of particular clans.

JOHO

Joho is the most spectacular part of the ritual sequence of *nimu cobi*. It is a competitive display put on by the clan of the deceased and the clans with which it is related by marriage. It begins with the representatives of the various clans parading around a horse-racing ground. The clan of the deceased goes in front, followed by those its daughters have married into and those of its daughters-in-law. In order to demonstrate the glory and magnificence of their own clan, the young men wear leather armor and carry knives, swords, and other weapons. They shout and dance, and strike military postures to demonstrate their clan's great name. The women wear their most beautiful clothes and put on their most valuable gold and silver jewelry, acting as if there were no one else present who could match their own display. The most magnificent boys and the most beautiful girls will be recognized easily from these parades. After the parades are over there is wrestling and horse racing. Those who distinguish themselves in wrestling and riding will be given prizes, many of which are offered spontaneously by onlookers who thus demonstrate their own wealth and generosity. Some people, after loudly boasting of their own clan and the worth of their prizes, will modestly say to an outstanding rider or wrestler, "I'm giving you this insignificant prize. Please accept it with a smile," but their real intention is to demonstrate their own pride.

[Translated by Stevan Harrell]

CHAPTER 8

Ghost Boards
and Spirit Pictures

BAMO QUBUMO

I T IS SAID THAT A LONG TIME AGO, BETWEEN HEAVEN and earth, at the very center of the world, there was a place that was hidden all year long by clumps of red clouds and sheets of white clouds. The gods in heaven and the people on earth could see this strange and beautiful place only when the red and white clouds were changing places. This place, called Shuzzur, was what we now call Liangshan.

In the spring of 1992, I returned from Beijing to the Liangshan homeland I had left a long time before, and chose as a research site Meigu County, the place where Nuosu culture is at its most dense and profound. One day, when I was on the early bus to Oquggu (Swan Village), I saw in the moving shadows outside the window that there were boards tied with strings to tree trunks. The white-haired elder seated next to me told me that they were ghost boards and narrated this myth about the origin of ghosts:

The time when heaven and earth were in chaos, the time of the six suns and seven moons, had already passed, and light was slowly emerging. The cock crowed for dawn, the swallows soared in the clouds, and the dawn was brightening. In the land of the Nuosu noble Ajy clan, the young men whistled up their hunting dogs to go to the mountains for the chase, and left for the forest. Responding to a dog's bark, a white river-deer was driven out of a bamboo grove. As the deer was fleeing, it butted into a world-famous hero in service of the Ajy clan, the warrior Hoyi Ddig-gur. No matter how the deer begged and cajoled, it could not stop the flight of Ddiggur's lethal arrow, and the arrow broke off the deer's neck and went directly through its tail. When the hunters ran to the place where the deer had fallen, they could not see the deer's shadow. They heard the sound of a hunting dog barking ahead of them, and when they went forward, following the sound, to investigate, they found the whole pack of hunting dogs barking around a clump of trees with red blossoms. As Ddiggur thought there was probably something hiding in there, he anxiously drew an arrow and shot into the trees. He hit a branch, which fell to the ground and disappeared, and standing in front of him was a maiden, the incomparably beautiful Zyzy Hninra.

One day Nzy Awo Nyiku, the head of another Nuosu tribe, took his hunting hounds to the forest to look for game and soon was face to face with Zyzy. He was stricken at first sight, and Zyzy Hninra followed Awo Nyiku to his clan's village, where the two lived happily together. The first year, Hninra was a beautiful wife, with a face like flowers and a bearing like the moon, and the second year she was a wise and capable spouse. But in the third year, Zyzy Hninra began to change—becoming nasty, evil, and cold—and people in the village began dying, one after

8.1. A *bimo* holding his *qike* in one hand while reading a ritual text. Note his hat, dress (Shynra style), and hero's belt.

58

another, for no apparent reason. In the fourth year, Awo Nyiku took ill. One day he asked about Zyzy Hninra's genealogy and origin, and she told him a plausible story. Awo Nyiku was very afraid and began to plot to control Hninra, and pretended that his illness was worsening. Hninra tried to cure him, and one day she turned into a red-winged kite and flew in an instant to an island in the middle of the sea to bring back a swan egg. Another day she turned into a banded jackal, and in the wink of an eye ascended a tall mountain, boring into a black bear's chest to steal the bear's gall bladder. Another day she changed into an otter and instantly dove to the bottom of a river to bring back a fish's heart. . . . But none of the medicines she brought back had any effect. One day Awo Nyiku said that with the exception of snow from the peak of the great mountain Minyak Konkar, nothing could cure him. Zyzy Hninra was determined to save her husband and decided that no matter what, she would go to that thousand-li-distant snowy mountain to fetch the snow.

After Hninra had left, Awo Nyiku quickly summoned ninety *bimo* from the upper end of the village and seventy *sunyi* from the lower end to his house to read texts and perform rituals. At that time, Zyzy Hninra had completed a thousand travails and was on her way back from the snowy peak, but because of the spells and curses of the *bimo* and *sunyi*, she slowly changed into a light-gray mountain goat with a red tail, and the snow that she had fetched for Awo Nyiku was still sticking to her hoofs, caught in her wool, stuck to her ears, and adhering to her horns. She knew her life was about over and wanted to ride the wind back home from the snowy mountain. She wanted to bring back the snow, to express her undying love for Awo Nyiku.

But Awo Nyiku summoned ninety young men and shot with an arrow the tired old goat, which they bound and took into a cave in the mountainside. Before long, the goat that Zyzy Hninra had been turned into was washed out of the cliffside cave into a river and fell into the cloth fishing basket of three herders from the household of Vusa Jjujjo, who, knowing nothing, skinned and ate it. As a result of eating the goat that Zyzy Hninra turned into, these people died and became ghosts who injure people everywhere.

Many tribes and clans were annihilated by the ghosts created by Zyzy Hninra, so the *bimo* and *sunyi* of every tribe and every clan all curse Zyzy Hninra with a thousand curses, and all say that Zyzy Hninra was the origin of ghosts.

When he had finished reciting the myth, the old man said that when Nuosu people invite *bimo* to their houses to perform rituals to exorcise ghosts, they always use goats as an exorcistic sacrifice, and on wooden boards they draw all kinds of ghosts and write all kinds of spells (fig. 8.2), so these are called "ghost boards," to show that the ghosts are

being expelled back to the ghostly realms, in the direction of the ghost mountain Ndabbu Lomo (in Ganluo County). Among the Nuosu-language ritual texts of the *bimo*, there is one called "The Ghost-Cursing Text" (also known as "Zyzy Hninra"), which has been transmitted all over Liangshan in verses with five- and seven-syllable lines. This text tells the story of the origin of ghosts, because in the Nuosu tradition, to exorcise ghosts one must first tell about their origin.

Thus began my fascination with ghost boards. Despite the warnings of Shyti, my young Nuosu assisant, that I shouldn't touch ghost boards or even look at them, I was

8.2. Ghost board (reverse side), with written spells against ghosts. (Photo by Bamo Qubumo)

able to collect some boards. I was not allowed to bring the ghost boards into our quarters and had to conceal them from the bus driver and passengers when I left the village (fig. 8.3).

From painted ghost boards I progressed to grass ghost dolls, clay ghosts, carved ancestral spirits, painted god pictures, and paper cutouts— all methods of imaging used by *bimo* in their rituals—and I began to inquire about the animistic beliefs and spirit worship of the people in the mountains, to think seriously about the meaning of each spirit picture or ghost board. Perhaps because of my obsession with ghosts, folks in the mountains gradually quit avoiding the subject and even gave me a special name, Ghost Bamo.

Rituals and Ritual Texts

Nuosu people believe that all disasters and illnesses are the result of meddling by ghosts, approaches by evil spirits, plagues of inauspicious influences, and the like. In order to ensure good harvests, healthy people, and healthy livestock,

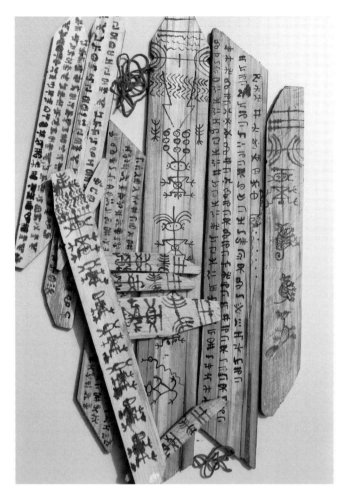

8.3. Ghost boards, showing front and back sides. (Photo by Bamo Qubumo)

ghosts and call benevolent spirits; *nyicy zze bi*, a ritual for cursing ghosts; and *cozze bi*, a ritual for cursing enemies. And since the ghosts that are being countered in these rituals are of all different sorts, they are repelled with specific rituals, such as those directed at expelling ghosts of young children, young unmarried women, and young unmarried men and ghosts that cause lingering illnesses, aphasia, minor illnesses such as colds and headaches, and specific illnesses such as leprosy. In Meigu most general rituals for protection against ghosts occur in the wintertime, since these rituals involve summoning spirits such as the gods of wind and rain, whose summoning in the summertime could have an adverse affect on crops. Ordinary ghost rituals, such as that for general cursing of ghosts that cause illness, can be completed in one night; more complex ones, such as those to expel ghosts that tie the body up, take two or three nights; and the most elaborate, designed to expel ghosts that cause lingering illnesses such as tuberculosis, may take as long as nine days.

As there are many rituals, so there are many texts, and those used by *bimo* are customarily classified into texts for offering, divination, or exorcism. Exorcism texts are further classified according to the type of ghosts they are directed against. Among over one hundred ritual texts passed on for generations in the lineage of the eminent *bimo* Qubi Shomo, for example, there are texts for sending off the soul, countering curses, cursing ghosts and enemies, curing diseases, exorcising the ghosts of unmarried women, fortune-telling, and divination of auspicious days, but texts of spells constitute a great portion. They are subdivided into thirteen categories, according to the kind of blood in which they are written and the kind of harm they are designed to cause or prevent. The most powerful among them, written in human blood, can cause quick death. These must be hidden in a cave and never brought into a house. Others, whose effects are somewhat less frightening, are written with animal blood or the venom of hornets.

For any ritual that involves a spell, a *bimo* must first read the text of *The Origin of Ghosts*, which tells the story of Zyzy Hninra, considered both a romantic myth and a charter story of the origin of ghosts. After this, the *bimo* summons his protective spirits and his many generations of ancestors, and proceeds with the particular texts germane to the specific ritual.

Ghost Boards and Incantations

Nuosu ghost boards are used in spells directed at ghosts. Before an exorcism ritual begins, it is necessary to make

people must invite *bimo* to perform rituals and recite texts to prevent natural and human disasters. Incantational texts, spirit pictures, and ghost boards are used in rituals to exorcise ghosts and prevent disasters, eliminate illnesses and avoid plagues, and cleanse pollution and eliminate defilement. Their ideological basis is entirely in exorcising ghosts and praying for good fortune, and their style of practice is always to use *bimo*'s incantations of texts that have sacred words and magical power, along with ritual behavior that can establish direct communication with spirits and ghosts. This communication enables people to control the ghosts and create talismans, which can transform danger into security and peril into safety, or prevent trouble before it happens.

Both rituals and the texts that accompany them are customarily classified into innumerable categories. For example, spells against ghosts include *xi'o bbur*, a springtime protection against evil spells; *jjyjo*, an autumn ritual to turn curses around; *yyrcy hlobba*, a wintertime ritual to exorcise straw ghosts (fig. 8.4), clay ghosts, and ghost boards. *Bimo* use bamboo pens, which they make themselves, and ink made of a mixture of the blood of sacrificial animals and black soot from the bottoms of pots to draw on the front side of prepared slabs of wood the ghosts to be exorcised. On the back they write the incantations and spells used for exorcism. When the ritual is almost over, the grass ghosts must be discarded and the ghost boards thrown away, to show that the exorcised ghosts have been expelled from the household. After the ritual is over, an assistant will take them to a road intersection and, facing in the direction of the ghost mountain Ndabbu Lomo, will hang them on a tree at the side of the road, to show that the ghosts have been sent back to the ghostly realms.

8.4. Straw ghosts. (Photo by Bamo Qubumo)

Ghost worship is a common religious activity among Nuosu. Every time the affairs of the household don't go smoothly, the harvest is bad, there is illness or injury, travels do not work out well, people cannot express themselves, there is fighting between households, or other troublesome situations occur, they are attributed to the lack of support from gods or to the malicious intentions of ghosts and demons, so a *bimo* must be commissioned to perform exorcisms and spells against ghosts, or a *sunyi* to become possessed by gods and drive out ghosts. The animistic orientation of the Nuosu has made worship of ghosts especially fervent, as Nuosu people not only believe in ghosts who inhabit the natural world—such as mountain ghosts, water demons, forest demons, cliff trolls—but in many categories of ghosts created through inauspicious deaths. These include the "infant ghosts" of children who died young, the "water ghosts" of people who drowned, and ghosts of hanged people. In addition there are headless ghosts, nine-headed ghosts, one-armed ghosts, and others. The prominence of ghosts in *bimo* thinking is quite remarkable. As Nuosu scholar Mosi Zzyhxo says, there are over two hundred kinds of ghosts mentioned in *bimo* texts from Liangshan. There are at least twenty different kinds of ghosts linked with insanity. Ghosts also come in many

shapes, such as the livestock ghost *tursha*, who has a long, thin nose and a cutting board hanging on his head, wears a sheepskin, and carries an axe in his hand and an old bamboo frame on his back. Animals afflicted by *tursha* may grow thin and die. The personalities and vices of ghosts are also quite various. For example, insanity-causing ghosts are fond of beauty and like to dress up. When they are being exorcised, one must present them with fancy and elaborate clothes, single- and double-edged combs, and pretty triangular lotus purses before they will agree to leave. So a *bimo* must command knowledge of ghosts and of the processes for manufacture of corresponding ritual implements and effigies. He must know the shape, peculiarities, and tastes of every kind of spirit, ghost, and demon—as well as the kinds of disasters and illnesses in production, social life, and health that each can inflict on people—before he can command spirits and ghosts through ritual, help people to court good fortune and avoid disaster, and guarantee the smooth progress and ultimate success of his rituals.

GHOST BOARDS IN THE EXORCISM
OF LEPROSY GHOSTS

In 1992, when I was randomly interviewing several tens of *bimo* and *sunyi*, respected old *bimo* Qubi Shomo, through his deep knowledge and broad learning, opened for me a great mountain pass to a realm of ghosts and spirits. He explained a large number of spells against ghosts and the texts that contained the spells. And a great *cur jy* ritual (for exorcising the ghosts of leprosy) conducted by nineteen *bimo* of Hxuogguluo Township displayed for me the uncanny and treacherous nature of ghosts.

To see this ritual, I climbed almost ten kilometers in driving rain on a mountain path to reach the ritual ground in a mountain hollow. The direct reason for this particular performance was that the house of a villager named Jjiejjie Zogi had been struck by thunder a few days before. In Nuosu thinking, anyone who encounters damage from thunder and lightning is sure to have something unfortunate happen. Thunder and lightning can transmit leprosy and other contagious diseases through trees and other media, so it is necessary to have a *bimo* perform the *cur jy* to expel the ghosts of contagious disease.

A *bimo* had divined that the auspicious time for the ritual was April 15, and the chief officiating *bimo* was Qubi Dage, with over ten other *bimo* assisting. The clients included eleven households in Jjolo Village who drew drinking water from a common spring; Jjiejjie Zogi was the chief client. On the evening of the 14th, each household that drank water from that spring had performed a small-scale *xi'o bbur* ritual to protect against evil spells, and the chief client's household had performed a larger *qocy yybi* ritual to exorcise ghosts. On the dawn of the 15th, each household brought the ghost boards of Curbu, the ghost of leprosy (which they had used in the spell-protection ritual the night before) to the place where the *cur jy* was to be performed. On the smoky ritual ground, the most noticeable thing was the ghost board used by the chief client's household: it was larger than the other ghost boards and lay on top of them (fig. 8.5).

On the front of this ghost board are, from top to bot-

8.5. Diagram of a ghost board for the *cur jy* ritual

tom, the nine-layered heaven, clouds and fog, moon and sun, constellations, lightning, trees, and the *cur* ghosts. The diagram as a whole shows the ghosts' creation among clouds, rain, thunder (implied), and lightning. The hordes of ghosts are distributed according to the three realms they inhabit in the heavens, in the empty spaces, and under the earth. On the left are the *cur* ghosts of heaven: from top to bottom, 1 is the nine-headed father ghost Curbu, who has nine heavenly transformations; 2 and 3 are the ghostly officials Jjie Ashy and Jjie Ahli, who command the thunder and lightning; and 4 and 5 are Dde Uoli and Dde Pazha, the ghostly servants of Curbu.

On the right are the *cur* of earth: 1 is the seven-braided mother ghost Curmo, who has seven earthly transformations; 2 is the hairless female ghost Ddeshy Suomo; 3 is the bald female ghost Dde Uonyie Suomo; and 4 is the broken-legged, bald female ghost Ddesi Suomo.

In the middle are the *cur* ghosts of the empty spaces, the sons and daughters of Curbu and Curmo: 1 is the one-armed ghost son Cursse Lodi; 2 is the one-eyed ghost daughter Curmo Nyuodi; 3 is the one-footed ghost son Cursse Xiedi; and 4 is the one-eared ghost son Cursse Hnadi.

Spirit Pictures

Spirit pictures are another important device used by *bimo* in their ritual contact with spirits and ghosts. The Yi creation story *Hnewo Teyy* tells of the hero Zhyge Alu, who shoots the suns and who was born at the dragon hour on the dragon day of the dragon month in the dragon year, the child of a dragon and an eagle. He has supernatural strength and special abilities to bring down magic and suppress ghosts, and is particularly fond of working for others' sake to root out harm and persevere on the rightful road. Stories and myths about him are told in every Nuosu household, by men, women, and children. In the spirit pictures drawn by *bimo*, his form dominates the structure. Strong, simple lines capture his magical powers and his strange and divine efforts to suppress ghosts.

Figure 8.6 shows Zhyge Alu as he frequently is seen in *bimo* ritual texts and in the spirit boards used in their ceremonies. In the middle is Zhyge Alu, with a copper helmet on his head; copper spear, arrow, and net in his hand; his head reaching as high as the sun and moon; and his feet astride the great earth. He cuts a majestic and imposing spirit figure, for in myth he is a great god who governs all extraordinary events in the human world. He is also the spiritual aid of *bimo* in their rituals to cure leprosy and to cast spells on ghosts and enemies alike. At the bottom of the picture is Zhyge Alu's nine-winged flying horse Symu Ddurndi, whose name means "long heavenly wings." It is said that he spends three days in heaven, three days on earth, and three days in the air, and that he can transform himself into clouds, thunder, rain, or snow. Zhyge Alu rides this horse to subdue ghosts and demons in heaven and on earth. Figure 8.7 depicts the spirit peacock Shoni Volie, who has a call like a snake. When snakes hear his voice, they congregate, and he eats them all up, so he is the heavenly enemy of snake ghosts. Figure 8.8 shows the huge python deity Baha, who eats snake ghosts and can swallow all the *cur* ghosts who cause leprosy.

When *bimo* use such spirit pictures in spells against ghosts, with the aid of Zhyge Alu's supernatural power they can subdue all ghosts and demons.

Nuosu people often commission *bimo* to draw such a picture on a wooden board to be used as a spirit plaque hung on the two sides of a doorway, to drive away ghosts and bring stability to the household. According to *bimo*'s explanations, the angular shape of Zhyge Alu's body illustrates the four earthly directions, and his copper helmet represents his struggles with the thunder spirits. The copper spear, arrows, and net are symbolic of his ability to subdue demons and conquer ghosts, because ghosts are afraid of copper. The supernatural birds and beasts are Zhyge Alu's spiritual helpers.

Zhyge Alu's spirit picture also covertly illustrates the myth of tribal origin that explains how Pumo Nieyyrmo became pregnant by thinking of eagle's blood and gave birth to Zhyge Alu. The conception and birth of an ancient tribe is crystallized cleverly in the spirit image, and it relates closely to the historical poem of the creation of the world, the *Hnewo Teyy*.

In addition to being inserted as static pictures in the texts of ritual spells employed by *bimo*, *bimo* spirit pictures are used dynamically in ritual performances. In Meigu County they are used primarily to curse leprosy ghosts, call souls, and to defend against leprosy.

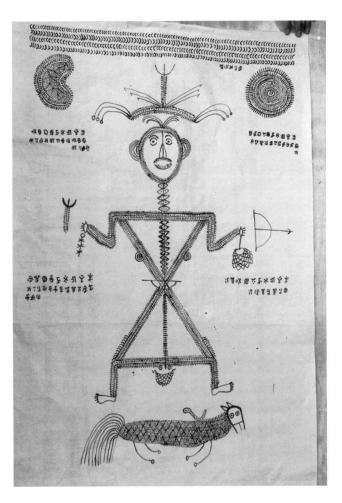

8.6. The spirit picture of Zhyge Alu, painted by *bimo* Qubi Shomo

8.7. The peacock Shoni Volie, one of Zhyge Alu's spirit helpers, painted by Qubi Shomo

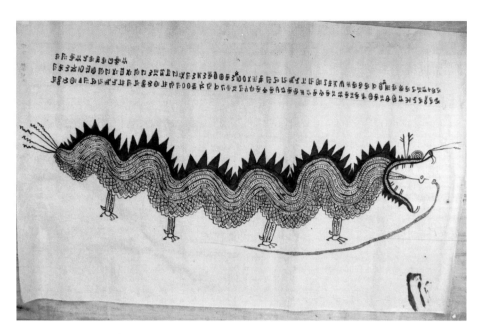

8.8. The python Baha, another of Zhyge Alu's spirit helpers, painted by Qubi Shomo

CURSING LEPROSY GHOSTS

Spirit boards are frequently used in rituals to curse leprosy ghosts. Leprosy is one of the most feared diseases among the Nuosu, who believe that *cur* ghosts are the cause of the disease. The ghosts appear amidst clouds, rain, thunder, and lightning in the form of creatures such as frogs, snakes, fish, otters, monkeys, and wasps, which invade human bodies and cause or transmit the disease. Anytime a village's residents experience chronic skin diseases, lighting strikes, or certain other omens appear, a ritual must be held to expel or prevent the entrance of the *cur* ghosts. *Bimo* without particular skills are usually unwilling to perform such rituals. Because the spirit picture of Zhyge Alu has the ability to defend against these *cur* ghosts, people often call it the "picture for defending against *cur*."

CALLING SOULS

Spirit pictures are often used in the ritual of calling souls, which is performed prior to the Nuosu New Year each fall. People often feel that at some point during their movements of the previous year—while traveling, herding, farming, hunting, and participating in rituals to send off the soul—their own soul might have left their body and remained out in the mountains. So they have a ritual performed to call back the soul and usually combine it with a general ritual to defend against evil spells. In such rituals,

bimo also include a section to defend against *cur*, using both the appropriate text and the "picture for defending against *cur*."

DEFENDING AGAINST LEPROSY

Spirit pictures are also used in a defensive ritual called *syryida*, which must be performed if people have relatives or ancestors who have been afflicted with leprosy. In preparation, people cut a cedar plank, called a spirit tablet, and draw on it all of the images of the Zhyge Alu spirit picture. They also cut a piece of black poplar wood into three pieces with jagged edges and tie it to the spirit tablet. They then carry out a small-scale counterspell ritual in which the *bimo* implants the counterspell in the wooden tablet and then takes the tablet around the house, tapping each person's head with it and in the end hanging it over the doorway of the main room of the house, to demonstrate its efficacy in suppressing and defending against *cur* ghosts. Afterward, the spirit tablet will be taken down and used again.

Many families ask *bimo* to draw a spirit picture on paper or wood so that at each New Year celebration, when pigs and sheep are killed, they may hang it over the host's place at the hearth. If *cur* ghosts are around looking for something good to eat, the picture's presence will prevent them from coming in.

[Translated by Stevan Harrell]